The Broad Concept Approach

The motto of Zlotnik, Lamb & Company:

'Advice is only as good as the person you ask.'

The Broad Concept Approach

HAROLD ZLOTNIK, CLU

Winning the Succession Game Inc.
Vancouver, Canada
2000

Copyright 2000 by Harold Zlotnik, CLU

All Rights Reserved
Unlawful to duplicate in any form or reproduce in whole or in part without prior written permission from the publisher.

Published by
Winning the Succession Game Inc.
Suite 1200 - 666 Burrard St.
Vancouver, BC
CANADA
V6C 2X8

Visit our site:
www.successionvideo.com

Cover design and illustrations by Alexandra Zlotnik

Publishing services provided by
New Star Books Ltd.
www.NewStarBooks.com

CANADIAN CATALOGUING IN PUBLICATION DATA

Zlotnik, Harold, 1922–
 The broad concept approach

ISBN 0-9687613-0-5
 1. Selling — Insurance. 2. Selling — psychological aspects. I. Title.
 HG8091.ZG6   368'.0068'8   C00-910896-3

To Nancy, my wife of 57 years

Contents

Preface · 9
Introduction · 11
What Is It That We Do? · 15
Human Capital · 19
The Broad Concept Interview · 25
The Sales Interview · 29
Assumptions · 35
The Five-Minute Coffee Interview · 39
The Role-Playing Advantage · 45
Estate Planning · 51
Rehearse Great Meetings · 61
Use Graphics · 65
Dealing With the Business Owner · 69
Telling a Story On Film — The Sturdy Family · 73
How Do You Handle Losing? · 83
How Do You Deal With the Gatekeeper? · 87
Does the 'Deal Killer' Really Exist? · 89
The Dream Merchants · 93
The Best Questions · 97
Know Your Business · 109
Summing Up · 115
Acknowledgments · 119
Biographical Sketch: Harold Zlotnik, CLU · 121

Preface

It is a great pleasure for me to dedicate this book, with love, to Nancy, my wife of 57 years. When she knew I was finally going to write this book she said, "Please tell your readers your formula for a wonderful life."

I said, "What's that?"

Nancy replied, "You know — tell them to learn how to make great lemonade."

As I look back over 54 years in the life insurance business, I realise that most of the value I have created for myself and others is a result of the lessons learned by making mistakes. My greatest weakness (or my greatest strength) is my willingness to believe that I can do anything that is possible, and when I fail and end up with a lemon, I usually learn a valuable lesson. Yes, I had to learn to make great lemonade.

In this book I hope to share what I have learned about this business and how to best serve our clients.

SPECIAL NOTE

Whenever I use "he" or "his," I respectfully submit this is to include she or hers. I have a great desire to see women reach their full potential in the business world and particularly as life insurance marketing professionals.

Introduction

I doubt that much of my thinking is original. In many cases, I don't know where the ideas have come from; however, over the years, I was fortunate enough to get to know three people who became my brains' trust.

The first is Joe Dickstein. Joe is a world-class thinker, and I credit him for introducing me to the Broad Concept-Style interview over thirty years ago. One of his associates was Don Pooley, who has been a speaker at the Million Dollar Round Table, and a brilliant exponent of that interviewing method. The third member of the group is Malcolm Scarratt, who coined the maxim that all of us, including my associates at Zlotnik, Lamb & Company, live by. He said, "There are two schools of thought in the marketplace. The first says, 'Do whatever you have to do to make the sale.' The second says, 'Do whatever you have to do to get the best job done for the client.'"

So how do you go through the process of helping the buyer get the best job done? Let's go through some of the key factors.

First we have to change the relationship. We should not see our role as selling insurance to the client; persuading him and educating him in order to make him see why he should buy life insurance. Rather we should sit by his side and help him determine what his issues are, what his concerns are and what his dreams are.

Our primary role is not to sell him, but to be his "buying consultant."

My attitude is (and has been since I got into this business) that the buyer is always smarter than he may appear to be. He has incredibly powerful antennae and can always sense where you are coming from. If you are anxious, he will know. If the focus is the sale itself, he'll know that too. If you care about doing the job right, he'll know, and if you are patient, he'll know.

We never lose the client while we're listening to him talk about his problems, his family, his business. We lose him when we get to discussing solutions too soon. When we patiently help him to understand the problems and to think about alternative solutions, he'll discover what is important to him and arrive at the point of wanting to take action so that his agenda is on the table and you can then work together towards the solutions, whatever they may be.

The client will enjoy this process because the whole discussion is in the area of his comfort level. He will also recognize that you are not trying to sell him. He will recognize that you are trying to help him to develop his agenda for his family, his business and the things he understands. Instead of you sitting across the desk trying to persuade him to act on your recommendations, you are sitting beside him, on the same side of the desk, as part of a team to determine the problems and what options should be considered as solutions.

As you go along, the client will develop a high level of trust towards you, which changes the process from being transactional to transformational. Trust is more than honesty and integrity. A very important ingredient is competence, which will lead the client to look at you as the key advisor, helping him to create his plan for his family and his business.

You are demonstrating your competence by asking questions

that help your client understand, not only the problems, but also the alternate solutions.

Another key element to this method is that you go into the first meeting and subsequent meetings with great confidence. This is simply because the sale is not the objective — the relationship is the objective. The client can sense this confidence and the usual buyer/vendor tensions aren't there on either side.

People are so often in the dark as to what they should do in this important planning area. To the extent that you can have a relaxing discussion and help him to turn on the lights, the relationship will flower.

So, the Broad Concept Approach, which I have been using for thirty-seven years, has allowed me to continue to enjoy our business. My role is that of a business guru and a relationship builder. This makes the business fun as well as profitable.

Therefore, the purpose of this book is to share what I have learned over years in the business. It has made me and my company successful, but more than that, it will help you position yourselves in the marketplace by offering a service that is unique and different than simply selling insurance or financial products.

I don't talk about theories. Instead, I talk about the things that I have actually done — things that you can do — that will enable you to sell more insurance and to have more fun.

Building relationships through trust and competence does not seem as fast a route to instant success as the transactional sale. Using the Broad Concept Approach, this book should help you to do whatever you have to do to get the best job done for your client.

*A service is always a relationship,
and a relationship is always a process.*

What Is It That We Do?

Periodically people ask me what I do, and it is not easy to tell them. I usually say that I get paid for selling life insurance, but that is not what I do. Their next question is, "Well, what is it that you do?"

I used to say that what I do is too difficult to explain and so I will have to show you. "Why don't we get together either next week or the following week over a cup of coffee and I will try to explain what I do by demonstrating how the particular area of planning I am involved in works."

Well, that is pretty awkward. However, it did get me many meetings, which resulted in quite a bit of business; but not too long ago I had lunch with a business client who really helped me to understand how to explain what I do.

This businessman, Martin, had been referred to me by one of my good clients, who is also a shareholder in Martin's business. I had sold insurance to the shareholders to cover their Buy-Sell Agreement, but I had never had a discussion with Martin on his overall planning. So one day I arranged a lunch with him for the sole purpose of discussing what I hoped would be the next stage in the process.

We had a delightful lunch, and Martin told me how much he thought of our mutual friend. We both knew our mutual friend had visited the Mayo Clinic in Phoenix each year as his way of getting an annual check-up. Then Martin started to tell me that recently he had taken his wife to the Mayo Clinic because they had difficulty getting a diagnosis here in Vancouver. Continuing with his story, he told me that after almost two days at Mayo, they had a diagnosis, and he was able to bring his wife back to Vancouver where she had the operation, which proved to be very successful.

I found Martin's story quite interesting because the Mayo Clinic can do it all. They not only do the diagnosis, but they have wonderfully trained surgeons who can perform the required operation. When you go through their system, you develop great confidence in their ability to do the job. Their motto is "Our only interest is the interest of the patient."

So after Martin told me the story of the Mayo Clinic he asked me, "So Harold, what is it you wanted to talk with me about today?"

Well, at that moment I had a flash of inspiration, and I said, "Martin, I wasn't quite sure how to explain it to you, but actually, you've just given me a clear explanation of what I wanted to talk with you about." Martin asked, "What do you mean?"

I answered, "Well, we have a financial Mayo Clinic."

"That's intriguing," Martin said, "Would you like to expand on that?"

I said, "Well, we spend 90 percent of our effort on the diagnosis, helping our clients to discover what the problems are. Once our clients understand the problems, the next part, the operation, as in your wife's case, is the easy part. The difficult part is finding out what is wrong."

Martin understood right away, and we made an arrangement to set up a series of appointments to get the diagnosis and planning done.

Maybe we have to work harder to come up with the right diagnosis, but the rewards are great. By using the Broad Concept Approach and asking probing questions, we help the client on a voyage of discovery where he himself is able to make the diagnosis. After all, it is his family, his business and his problem. Our role is to help him to discover his answer and his solution. He may fight our answer. He may question our answer. But he will always buy in to his answer when he understands.

Human Capital

Most insurance transactions of any size today are based on hard facts, an examination of the tax liabilities and other related costs when a man dies. These facts may be to fund a Buy-Sell Agreement between shareholders or to clear a debt obligation or to pay taxes. In each case, it is an accounting procedure, crunching numbers to determine the amount of insurance required.

This doesn't place a value on the life of the insured. It determines the hard fact of the size of the problem when a man dies.

Now, let's come at this from a different perspective. Let's assume we are dealing with a business owner or significant shareholder or CEO. What is the real value to the company of this HUMAN LIFE asset, this human capital? If you look at the operating statement, you will see that the only reference to this human asset is as a liability for the expense of carrying that executive. So this key player isn't even shown as an asset. If you were to try to assess the value of the body parts it would come to about nine dollars (at least that is not a liability).

Let's assume that the key player was hit by a truck and killed and the offending driver was found negligent. How much would the family sue for? Probably it would be in the millions, and the family would win. Why? What changed the value of this bag of bones? Usually it's an assessment of future earning potential. We are talking about the value to the family, but the major monetary loss is to his company. How big is this loss?

The potential loss here is staggering. Let's talk about it, because now we are dealing with soft facts. Let's look at a few examples.

The first is the business owner who has a license or franchise. One condition of the franchise is that on the death of the owner, the franchiser agrees to buy the business back for cash. This is not an unusual arrangement. There are many franchise-style agreements that can be a problem on the death of the franchisee, because in many cases the buy-back occurs at book value.

Here is a real example. Mr. M owned a distributorship with a top brand manufacturer. His business had been very successful and its earnings had reached two million per year before tax. Based on earnings, the business would be valued in the ten million dollar range. However, on his death it was to be sold back to the manufacturer for its book value of less than two million. Through the miracle of life insurance he could have his ten million dollar value insured. The rest is a detail of tax and technical planning. If Mr. M wanted that full ten million to go to his family, it was within his control to make that happen.

Now let's change just one important detail. Mr. J has a contracting business. He's very successful. He has a great executive team and his wife is involved in the administrative part of operations. It is not a distributorship so there is no buyer sitting in the wings (that is an important detail). Here is the way the discussion went:

The meeting was with Mr. J and his wife. Mr. J and his wife are in their late fifties. They are modern, capable entrepreneurs who focus on planning and doing things right. Their son has worked in the business and has the ability to one day run the business and be the successor. But that day is probably ten years away. Mr.

J has built a management team including Ken, a forty year old, who has handled major projects.

Our initial discussions have involved estate planning, trusts, death, taxes, and the fact that one of the lenders has the assignment of two million dollars of insurance on Mr. J's life. In the meeting, both Mr. J and his wife are very open about where they are and what plans they have for the future. The insurance is sufficient to pay the bank and the death taxes and leave Mrs. J with about one million in cash along with the business.

I then ask them this question, "What was the last important business decision the company had to make?" Mr. J responds, "We're just completing a government contract for the next three years. That was a big decision."

"Who was at the meeting from your company?" I asked. He replies, "Ken my General Manager, Bill, one of my road building superintendents, and I." I then say, "Could the deal have been done without you there?" He says, "I think so but there would be some slippage. It wouldn't have been the same deal." So I say, "And before that, what was the last big decision?" He says, "That's easy, hiring Ken, the General Manager." I say, "OK who was at that meeting?" And Mr. J says, "My wife and I." So I pause for a few moments and say, "There's a thought running through my head that I would like to share with both of you." "What's that?" they ask. "Well," I say, "If I were a shareholder in this company, I would want to see ten million dollars of insurance on Mr. J at least for the next ten years."

Now I don't usually volunteer my answer, I usually let the client discover his answer, but my two questions sent a strong message that this company could lose great opportunities if Mr. J died too soon. It also sent a message that the important issues weren't the hard facts (details that can be measured such as taxes, debt, etc.). The major issue was loss of opportunity — loss of human life value. It was obvious to me and I helped make it obvious to them that we probably couldn't buy enough insurance to pay for his loss!

What do these two cases illustrate? Let me again volunteer my thoughts.

My first thought is that the buyer is much more ready to buy than we are ready to sell. There's nothing wrong with that. We should always learn from the buyer. If this assumption is right then we have an awesome responsibility. In a time in history where the dedicated life producer is in danger of becoming extinct, the buyers are telling us that we aren't even close to satisfying the needs of the marketplace for life insurance.

How many companies are there today which have a value of anywhere from one million to 100 million where the principal player is the major asset of the company? If we ask the questions: "What was the most important decision this company has made recently?" "Who was at the meeting where that decision was made?" we are zeroing in on the real values in the company: the values of its key decision-makers!

Maybe you're already doing this, but it's not what we hear discussed in any depth at industry meetings.

My next thought is that people in business like to identify a problem and then solve it. We're talking about a problem they can see and can feel, and assuming the person is insurable, a problem that they can solve. It isn't complicated. They can always do the complicated stuff later.

This is where we're at our best — we are dealing with the soft facts of fears, feelings, and emotions; soft facts that the technicians find so difficult to deal with. However, to me, the soft facts are the ultimate simplicity. It is insuring the key values in any successful organization without getting complicated. We are talking the language of business, which is how decisions are made.

One of the key elements of these discussions is to ask the kinds of questions that involve the client in the problem. There is a Chinese proverb that says, "Tell them and they may forget. Show them and they may remember. Involve them and they will understand." Though the questions may be simple, they have the purpose of involving the client in whatever problems we were discussing. The great value of this type of discussion is its simplicity.

When we're successful we are taking that nine dollar man and putting a real value on him. We can get excited about that!

The Broad Concept Interview

It started back in September 1945. I had just returned from service overseas with the Royal Air Force. While overseas I had been awarded the Distinguished Flying Cross, but back in Vancouver I had only thirty days to find a job because that was the length of time the Air Force paid you before you became a civilian once more.

My father had been a jeweller, and it must have been in the Zlotnik genes, because the English translation for "Zlotnik" is "Goldsmith". My father had passed away in 1943, but it was assumed I would join a good friend of his who was a jewellery wholesaler. Full of high hopes that I would soon have a new job to support my wife Nancy, my son Marty and myself, I went to see my friend Ralph. When he explained that the factories in Switzerland weren't shipping any merchandise because the returning servicemen were the first priority of North American-bound ships, I was back on the street looking for a job.

My father had left my mother the proceeds of a small life insurance policy. I was persuaded by her to go and present myself to the local office of the insurer who had paid her those proceeds. Three days later I was in the life insurance business.

I was twenty-three years old with only a high school education, and knew nothing about business or economics, but I liked the idea of selling. My first day on the job I found out that the manager of this insurance office had recently quit because he didn't believe in life insurance. A supervisor gave me a three-inch thick black book containing rates and values for all the plans being offered, and that completed my training.

As I looked around the office that first morning, I saw four of the agents over in a corner playing bridge. I already knew how to play bridge. What I needed was someone to show me how to sell life insurance. It was my lucky day. I was sitting at my desk trying to decide what to do next, when Percy, a tall, gangly, genial agent walked over and asked if I would like to spend the day with him going on calls. I would soon find out what he meant.

Fifteen minutes later we were in my car, headed for a residential area where there were many young families. However, along the way I needed to stop and get some gas so we pulled into a service station. It wasn't self-service in those days, and as the attendant started filling my gas tank I got into a conversation with him. I don't remember what I said, but I think I asked him if he had life insurance. When he said, "No," I wasn't sure what to say next, so I called Percy out of the car, and ten minutes later we had completed an application for a $5,000 whole life policy. As we were driving down the highway I asked Percy what had happened, and he said, "Harold, you've just made $100." I was so excited I just couldn't wait to get home and tell Nancy. You see, my draw in September 1945 was $250 a month and I had just made $100 in under an hour. It was a great thrill!

The formula for success in those early days was deemed to be a weekly schedule of fifty calls to produce ten interviews to produce two sales, and somehow or another, I managed to accomplish this. Over the next few years I went to many meetings, learned as much as I could and became a very good presenter. It is hard to believe that it is now over fifty-four years later.

This book is also about the transition over those fifty-four years, from "good presenter" to "good listener." I was lucky to make that transition from presenter to listener and communicator. It all happened because I joined a small company of super-producers. When I joined this company I met the two principal proponents of a new method of interviewing called The Broad Concept. I have spent the last thirty years learning to use this concept in my personal and business life. It is a way of communicating more effectively by asking questions and developing your listening skills.

The benefits I have enjoyed have been more fun, more money, more clients versus customers, more respect, better relationships, more confidence and more fulfilment. At seventy-seven years of age I am still having that fun and enjoying the interviews and continuing to learn how to do it better. Although I don't go into my office as much as I used to, every business day is still exciting for me.

So what is this Broad Concept Approach anyway?

The last hundred years has belonged to the great presenters, and I believe the next hundred years will belong to the great communicators, and part of that learning to be a great communicator is learning the broad concept.

The main facets of the broad concept interview are:

1. Ask, don't tell.

2. Eighty percent of the discussion should involve listening and only twenty percent is talking.

3. Ask soft-fact questions.

4. Discover feelings and attitudes.

5. Discuss concepts, not details.

6. Spend ninety percent of the time discussing the client's problems and only ten percent on solutions.

7. It's the client's family, business and problems. Help the client to develop his own solutions.

8. Patiently help the client to understand.

The Sales Interview

The interview is to the sale what the golf swing is to the game of golf. Maybe one can improve their score in golf by getting a new set of tools (or clubs), and maybe one can improve their sales by focusing in on a new product or a lower rate. But the long-term benefits of perfecting the interview far outweigh any of the alternatives.

When we are dealing with high net worth clients, business owners, senior executives and successful professionals, what should be the objective of the interview? Generally, it should be to develop the relationship patiently so that, as the process continues, the result is a series of interviews. The objective is to establish a client relationship.

Since these interviews are with very busy and highly focused people, it is necessary to find the client's comfort level as early as possible. It is also very important to know that the client is listening. There is one extremely effective way of accomplishing this, and that is to ask questions.

If you are talking, you may think the client is listening, but people are very adept at faking this response, and we have no way of knowing what they are really thinking. It is like we are transmitting, but the other party's receiver may have been turned off. One way to make sure that the receiver is turned on is to have the client take an active role in the process through asking him questions. Our role is to listen carefully to those responses and then ask the client questions that relate to those responses in order to help us to understand the client's feelings, concerns and objectives.

It is critical that we work with the client to develop his agenda. This is best accomplished by asking a set of questions, which help him to establish what that agenda is. However, if it is a first interview, we can't jump right in and fire off a series of questions. There first must be an opportunity for the client to talk about where he has been, where he is and where he is going. Therefore, one of your first questions may be, "How did you get started in this business?" Usually the answer to this question takes twenty minutes to a half hour or more, and it helps you to understand where this client is coming from, how difficult the early years were and how importantly he treats each facet of his business. He usually talks about feelings as well as the facts, so this will give you some insight into what kind of person he is. Often this one question and the answers set the stage for what the business person wants his agenda to be.

Believe it or not, most business owners are lonely. Most of them don't have anybody they can really confide in. For example, if they told their families about some of the financial issues involved in the business, they might scare them to death. They can't talk about some of the important problems facing the company or they might frighten their senior employees. If they discuss some of the same problems with the lender, they might expose themselves to some serious consequences. But here we are, unthreatening, interested and willing to listen. By listening we are paying him the greatest compliment. We are telling him that what he has to say is very important.

Sometimes he tells us that a few years back he hired this great manager and that he is getting the chance to get out and play a little more golf and foresees the possibility of getting more time off in the not-too-distant future. He might also tell us about one of his kids who is working in the company and is being groomed for possible succession. When each of these issues come up, I like to ask questions and get him to expand on his thinking: questions such as, "How would that work?" "Would you want the manager to have a stake in your company?" "Would you want your son/daughter, who is going to be your successor, to have a stake in the company?"

Gradually, as we discuss these questions, we are honing in on what his position is today. I may then ask a few question such as, "You have been very successful. What are your main concerns today?" "What do you see as your greatest opportunity?" I may also ask, "Where do you see the company five years from now?" "How do you see your role?" "How do you see the role of the manager?" "How do you see the role of your son who is going to be your successor?" This discussion may take one to two hours, and it is a discussion where I am doing maybe ten to twenty percent of the talking and he is doing eighty to ninety percent of the talking. I am listening and learning, and as he is telling me his story, he is also learning. He is remembering the challenges and difficulties he has overcome to get to where he is today. He is thinking about where he wants to go in the future, and he is focused.

At some point in the discussion, I am going to discuss his priorities, which are: Family first, Business second, Creditors and taxes last.

Let me emphasize: this is not a manipulative technique. It is a reasoned, accurate way of helping the client to determine what the issues are and what he should be thinking about. I give him no answers and no proposals, and at the end of that one or two hours I will say something to this effect: "Look, it has been most interesting talking with you today, and I think I am beginning to get a feel for what you are trying to accomplish. Let's get

Priorities: Family first, business second, creditors and taxes last.

together again in ten days or two weeks when we both have had a chance to think about things. At that meeting we may be able to establish some firm objectives and some alternatives for accomplishing those objectives."

I really don't have to say that much, and I almost always get that second meeting.

A number of important things have happened in this first interview. First, I have established a role as facilitator or consultant rather than one as salesman. Second, I have given the client the opportunity to talk about the things that are most important to him. Third, I have made him feel good — I have listened to him. Fourth, important questions have been asked, but no solutions have been proposed. Thus, the client's interest has been greatly aroused. Fifth, by not proposing answers and patiently developing the relationship, I have established a position of respect with the client. Sixth, and most important, I have identified conceptually what the process is, which is "putting his family first."

Just think, these problems have developed over many years. If I give him a fast solution, how much credibility would I have? It would be like going to visit your doctor and telling him you have a severe pain in the abdomen. However, if he prescribes medication without giving you a thorough examination, how much respect would you have for that doctor?

Remember, there is no such thing as "the right answer." The key is to develop and to try and understand the main problems, and then to look at alternate solutions. Prescription without an examination and proper diagnosis is malpractice, whether it is in the field of medicine or in the field of life insurance.

Assumptions

My lifetime home, Vancouver, is a very beautiful city. On the northwest side of the city are mountains, and up the side of one of these mountains is a scenic golf course called the Capilano Golf and Country Club. One summer day a crusty old senior member was walking down from the clubhouse to the first tee where he saw a man addressing the ball about six inches in front of the markers. He walked over to him, and in a somewhat supercilious voice said, "My good man, don't you know the rules of golf? You are supposed to be playing from behind the markers." To which the golfer looked up with some annoyance and said, "Look, in the first place, I am not your good man. In the second place, yes, I know the rules of golf, and in the third place, this happens to be my second shot."

Well, we are all trapped in our assumptions from time to time. But there are a number of assumptions we can use that may help in terms of your attitude to the business of selling life insurance.

The seven assumptions are:

1. Everybody loves somebody or something (sometimes it's the business).

2. Mortality is one hundred percent per person.

3. Most people die leaving a need for cash.

4. The most certain and economic way of providing cash at death is life insurance.

5. People think with their heads, but they act with their hearts.

6. If they understand, they may act.

7. If there is a sense of urgency, they will act.

By far the most important assumption is "people think with their heads, but they act with their hearts." Think of the major decisions you have made in your life. Were they made logically or emotionally? Was the decision to get married a logical decision? (Don't ever tell your spouse it was a logical decision.) What about your decision to buy a house? Was that decision made logically or emotionally? (There is no question that logic plays a part and helps to back up the emotional decision.)

The age of computers has brought wonders of efficiency to our business. We can now design a policy exactly to our clients' wishes in a matter of minutes. It used to take weeks to get this information. However, the computer has also created a major trap. The creation of the computer printout has made it easier to focus on the details of the policy rather than on the importance of diagnosing the problems or problem to be solved.

People don't need to know what an insurance policy is — they need to know what an insurance policy does. So how do we get the needs of the client back into focus? One of the facets of the broad concept is to concentrate on the jugular issues, or the broad issues, and not on the details, or capillary issues.

In the same way that the client has to realign his thinking and approach to estate planning and develop a conceptual set of objectives, we as professional salespeople have to develop a concept about our role.

First, as professional salespeople, I think we should be proud of the part we play in the success of our economy and our country. If we go back a few years, it would have been easy to recognize that there were two major powers on the world scene. In those days it was the USSR and the USA, and we all know what happened. The USA developed as the leading economic power in the world and the USSR disintegrated into a number of states that are currently dealing with major economic problems. What you may not have made note of, however, is that there were no salespeople in the USSR. They simply produced products for the marketplace, and hoped that those products would sell. In many cases there were great shortages because there was underproduction, and in many cases there were supplies that died on the shelves because the products didn't meet the needs of the people.

   One of the great roles of professional salespeople in our society is that, not only do they market the goods and services that are available, but they also meet with their customers and clients. Professional salespeople act as a conduit for what the marketplace really wants. It is that feedback from professional salespeople that helps drive the research and innovation of successful companies.

   The best professional salespeople have an attitude, and this is best described by talking about the two schools of thought in the marketplace. The first school of thought believes that you do whatever you have to do to make the sale. The second school of thought believes that you do whatever you have to do to satisfy the needs of the client. It is those who subscribe to the second school of thought that I would describe as "true professional salespeople." Those true professional salespeople know that the best way of determining how to deal with their clients' needs is to ask questions. They deal with concepts, not products. They work with and employ technicians; they don't act like technicians themselves.

   Because they ask questions, they are usually dealing with the most important and valuable issues that represent the clients' concerns. I like to express this as dealing with jugular issues rather than capillary issues. Let's discuss some of these jugular issues.

1. The financial security of the client's family.
2. A long-term strategic plan for the client's business, which includes making sure it is financially healthy.
3. A plan to clear the estate by dealing with the tax collector and the creditors.

As professional salespeople, our role is to work with the client, help him to define his objectives and then deal with these jugular issues.

We help the client to solve these jugular problems, and not because of our great technical skills, tax knowledge, insurance knowledge, or where we find the lowest priced products. We help him to solve these problems by virtue of our skills as communicators. Professional salespeople must be excellent communicators.

You very seldom ever find that a business owner will tell you that he doesn't understand. After all, if he runs a successful business, he is supposed to be knowledgeable about almost everything. Yet, when a technical discussion takes place in an interview, if you watch carefully, you may see your client's eyes glaze over. However, you will never lose him when you talk about his family and his business. You never lose him when you ask questions and let him have the role he deserves, which is that of the main player in the planning process.

The life insurance policy may be the solution, but what is the problem? An analogy is to say that there are thousands of pills, but what is the illness? We have discussed the role of the professional salespeople, and one of the key elements is asking questions. An example of this is the five-minute coffee interview.

The Five-Minute Coffee Interview

Bill, who is a young architect of about thirty-five, and I have been sitting over a cup of coffee for about ten minutes. Finally I ask him the following question:

"Bill, do you have a will?"

"Yes," he replies.

I say, "Well, tell me what it says."

And if Bill does not have a will, I have learned something, haven't I? In that case I would probably say something like this, "Well, Bill, if you had a will what would it say?"

In any case, Bill has a will and he answers, "I leave everything to my wife."

I ask, "What is everything?"

Bill says, "Well, I have the house, the car, a few investments and some life insurance."

And I say, "Bill, if you had died last night, what does your wife do with all that?"

Bill asks, "What do you mean?"

I respond, "What I mean is this. Does she get an income, or does she start cashing in her assets? Just how does she handle the whole thing?"

Bill says, "Of course I would want her to have an income."

I say, "How much income?"

Bill says, "Well, let's see ... about $30,000 to $40,000 per year."

I then ask him, "Is that to spend, or does she have to pay taxes on that amount?"

Bill responds, "Well, at $40,000, she'd have some tax to pay. I think I'd like her to have $40,000."

And I say, "Bill, if I'd asked you that question five years ago, what would the answer have been?"

Bill thinks for a minute and then answers, "Well, about five years ago, the answer would have been about half: about $20,000."

I ask him, "Do you think inflation is going to continue?"

Bill answers, "Of course."

And then I will probably ask the most important question of all. I ask him, "Bill, how important is it to you that your wife gets that $40,000 per year? How important is it?" I get almost the same answer, word for word, every single time.

Bill says, "Damned important!" (Obviously a man who loves his wife.)

I then say, "OK, how much capital would you have to have to produce $40,000 of income?"

Bill responds, "Well, if I understand your question, at roughly five percent interest I think I would need a little over $800,000." Now, up to this point I haven't given Bill any answers. I am simply asking questions. He is educating me and at the same time, educating himself. He is doing the thinking. His receiver is on and he is transmitting and can feel the problem.

I then say, "That sounds about right. Are you expecting to inherit any money in the near future."

"No," says Bill.

I then ask, "How much capital do you have now that can be used specifically to produce income?"

Bill answers, "Well, let's see. I have $250,000 of insurance, $25,000 in my company pension plan and I have another $25,000 in investments, cash, etc. That comes to about $300,000."

I say, "Well, let's see now. How much are you short?" This is the moment of discovery isn't it?

Bill starts to figure. He says, "$800,000 is what is needed, minus the $300,000 that I have. That leaves $500,000, which is what I am short. I need $500,000."

I then ask him, "Where are you going to get $500,000 in a hurry, Bill?"

Bill says, "You son-of-a-gun! And how much would life insurance cost?"

Now I haven't made any statements. I haven't proposed anything. I have simply asked questions. I haven't judged any of his answers and it has taken about five minutes. The coffee interview is a very simple interview. Let's discuss what happened.

A famous sales trainer, Lee Dubois, tells us that once the client has given you a buying signal, you have to let him know he has bought. That is the purpose of a closing question.

Bill's question, "How much would life insurance cost?" is a buying signal, isn't it? There are times when I might answer that question by just saying, "Two percent." Or I might say, "Well, the maximum cost will be $500,000, because that is the size of the problem, isn't it? And if you can't get that insurance, that's the cost. Now the alternative is depositing two percent to your own insurance account. But that is not really a cost, is it?"

Also, I relate the cost as a percentage rather than giving him the amount of the premium. In effect, what he is doing is paying interest to create capital.

Another concept is that we really don't have to be concerned about what the prospective client's answer is. After all, we are not really selling him insurance. In this case, the cost is

$500,000 until somebody shows him an alternative that costs less.

Remember that Bill told me it was very important that his wife have these funds. So the trade off here is a $500,000 premium if he does nothing versus two percent per year if he uses insurance.

Remember when I asked Bill how much income would his wife have needed five years ago? Well, in many interviews I will also ask, "If I were to ask you that question five years from now, what will your answer be?"

Now we are getting into the concept of projecting the problem, and it is important, because if Bill doesn't get hit by a truck on his way out of the medical examiner's office, he is probably going to be around for quite some time. If Bill passes the medical, what's the point of solving his needs at today's figures?

I will try to get the client to see this and buy the solution, assuming he lives another five years. The worst that can happen is that he won't try to reduce the $500,000 of capital he needs today. It is amazing how often the client will buy at that level of the projection, even if that additional coverage is just term coverage.

Now there may be other issues we can deal with later, but he has made a decision on the most important question. Bill has a wife and two kids, and that income is going to mean that they are taken care of. My friend, Don Pooley, talks about "soft fact" questions, which deal with feelings and attitudes. The "hard fact" questions are those which deal with numbers, assets, etc. "How important is this to you?" is a powerful "soft fact" question.

One of the things I've mentioned is how dangerous it can be to make assumptions about the buyer. One of the most widely held assumptions by people who are in contact with the business owner, his family, his employees, his competitors, etc., is that somehow, because of the quality of his advisors and because of his success in business, the business owner must have devel-

The Five-Minute Coffee Interview • 43

Hard facts deal with numbers and assets.

Soft facts deal with feelings and attitudes.

oped a very good, workable estate plan. This is not only a dangerous assumption, but it is one that may often lead to a great deal of tragedy.

In fact, the vast majority of business owners and entrepreneurs fail to have a viable estate and succession plan in place when they die.

The Role-Playing Advantage

Sometimes I role-play with the business partner because whatever his answers are, he becomes fully involved in the problem. Also, it brings a sense of urgency to the situation, doesn't it? And this sense of urgency answers one of the biggest objections we get when a man says, "I want to think about it."

He is really answering that way because, first, he doesn't understand, and second, there is, to his mind, no sense of urgency. That is why role-playing is so very effective.

As far as I'm concerned, role-playing has another great advantage. Since I am asking the questions (and know beforehand what these questions are), I can stay quite relaxed. In fact, I'm acting much the same way Columbo did in those television sequences a few years ago. He walks along in his beige raincoat and just asks a few seemingly innocuous questions — and at the end of each sequence, the "clever" criminal is having handcuffs put on and dazedly marches off to jail.

It can be done. You can learn to be effective in role-playing by trying it out in the privacy of your home. The key is developing the right questions to ask. Also, it's important to get the client involved in the development and understanding of the problem and in thinking out his own solution to that problem. To the extent that this is done, objections should not come up.

Here is an example of role playing with two businessmen:

I am meeting with two prospective clients, Harvey and Tom, who have a business, H&T Manufacturing Inc. The business is quite successful and growing nicely, and they have determined the company to have a current value of $2,000,000. They each own fifty percent of the shares. Harvey doesn't have a will. Recently he had a very interesting experience. He went to visit his lawyer and he started to discuss his will. When the lawyer asked him about the business, and Harvey indicated to the lawyer that he had fifty percent of the shares of H&T, the lawyer said "Harvey, I'm sorry, I can't draw your will." When Harvey asked, "Why not?" the lawyer said. "What would your wife and kids do with fifty percent of the shares in a private company? Your family needs to know that they are going to receive cash for your interest in the company, and that cash can be invested to produce income. Once this has been done we are then in a position to draw up a will that makes some sense."

Harvey's lawyer recognized that his role was more than acting as a legal technician to draw up documents. He wanted to know that the documents would have a purpose and that whatever will was drawn would be properly financed and would work to carry out Harvey's wishes for his family.

Now it's a few days later and Harvey, Tom and I are in a meeting to discuss their respective interest in the company and the potential for a buy-sell agreement to be financed through life insurance.

I say to Tom and Harvey, "Look, gentlemen, it would be quite helpful if we could do some role-playing in order to highlight some of the issues that need to be dealt with." They both say,

"OK. Let's see where that takes us." (The meeting is taking place in Harvey's office.)

The next thing I say is, "Harvey, I would like to make two assumptions. The first is that you died last night and the second is that I am your executor. Now I would like to trade seats with you. I'll sit in your chair and I'd like you to come over here, and you are now out of this conversation. Remember the assumptions, I am your executor and you died last night. I will now carry on a conversation with Tom. Keep in mind, Harvey, that I am representing your interests as your executor. OK?" So Harvey changes places with me and I say to Tom, "As Harvey's executor I am dealing with his estate, and I have to report back to his family on the status of his interest in the company. The first question I have is, have any arrangements been made to deal with Harvey's shares?"

Tom says that he is not aware of what all the options are, except that he knows that they have a provision whereby if the shares are to be sold, they first have to be offered to the other shareholder.

So I say, "Assuming that after I meet with the family within the next day or two and they do decide to sell the shares, can you write a cheque for $1,000,000?"

Tom says, "You and I both know the answer to that. I don't know where I can get hold of $1,000,000 in a hurry. I don't think I want to go into debt even if it were possible to borrow that much. I guess the only option would be to work out some way to pay the estate out over a period of years."

At that point Harvey puts his hand up and I say, "What is it Harvey?" He says, "I'm dying to get back into the conversation." I say, "Sorry, not yet, Harvey. Remember what we agreed to regarding the two assumptions. The first is that you died last night and the second is that I am the executor of your estate. If that's the case, then I have to deal with these issues without you."

So Harvey settles back in his chair and I again turn to Tom. I then say, "Tom, let's assume that you're going to buy this company. What period of time do you think you would need in order to be able to pay off that $1,000,000?"

Tom says, "Well, I'd like to do it over five years, if possible."

So I ask, "Well, how much capital is that per year?"

Tom says, "$200,000 per year."

I then ask, "Would there be interest involved?"

Tom says, "Well, we'd have to negotiate that. Let's assume it would be the same interest I would have to pay a bank."

I say, "OK, so it's something more than $200,000 a year. Would you be planning to take that money out of the company in order to make a payment?"

Tom says, "I'm not sure whether the company could buy back the shares. Let's assume I would have to draw the money out and then pay Harvey's estate."

I then say, "Let's assume that you have to have $200,000 plus the interest. How much does the company have to pay you so that you can pay the income tax and have enough left over to make the payment each year?"

Tom says, "Well, whether I take it personally or whether the company buys back the shares, the number is going to be a lot more than $200,000 per year. It would take virtually all of our income, and that's why we wanted to get together with you and go over some alternatives to come up with a game plan that will work."

I say, "But, Tom, remember the two assumptions. Harvey died last night and I am his executor. If that's the case we don't have a chance to change the game." I then turn to Harvey and say, "OK, Harvey, let's get back to our original seats and let's talk about what can be done that will be a workable game plan."

We're there, aren't we? The rest of it is just details.

Usually Harvey will say something like this, "When I was sitting there I was thinking about some of the issues, and one of the things that occurred to me is that if Tom was going to pay me over a few years, what would you do as executor if one of the payments was missed? What would be your recourse?"

I respond by saying, "One cannot know what the answer is. Let's look at some of the questions the executor might have under those circumstances. Would one of his questions be, 'Do I sue Tom?' There would be great danger in doing this. First of all, you cannot be sure that the suit is going to be successful, but you do know that it will be costly. Second, it could drag on over a considerable period of time, and if Tom were having trouble paying, it might put the company in a more hazardous position. Third, if you were successful but Tom didn't have any assets, what you would get back is the shares. This raises a whole series of other questions such as: 'Do you wind the company up?' 'Do you try to run it?' These are not issues that an executor would like to get involved in. These are the very reasons why it is important to have a firm buy-sell agreement in place, clearly outlining terms and conditions of the transactions. It also shows the importance of financing it using life insurance. In this way the event that creates the problem creates the cash at the lowest cost to provide the solution when it is required the most."

As you can see, role-playing helps to create a sense of urgency and also brings a degree of clarity to the problem. Both shareholders now are aware that the problem exists, and it is one they want to get rid of and to solve as quickly as possible. Because there is a sense of urgency, they are going to push me to get that job done.

The other thing about role playing is that it brings a higher degree of interest and provides some fun in the process.

Estate Planning

I wish the phrase "estate planning" had never been coined, as it is very misunderstood. For many business people and their advisors, the concept of estate planning is confused with tax planning.

Estate planning is deciding what you want to happen when you die and making sure that it does happen.

What is an estate plan? The only valid estate plan a person dies with is their last will and testament. Transfers at death are governed by what is said in the will. The "testator" (the person who is the subject of the will) has set out his wishes in a binding legal form. The will is also the last message that he or she will ever leave to their spouse, family, friends, employees, etc. Therefore, it is a terribly important message.

How much thought should go into this very important message? Who will be affected by this message?

Most business owners would be horrified if they could come back a few days after they died to witness the unresolved problems they left behind. It has been said that most businessmen spend more time getting their hair cut during a year than they spend on this very important process, which involves the survival of their families, their businesses and even their employees.

The purpose of the will is to set out the transfer of assets in the most effective way possible. The first clause of the will states, "I hereby instruct my executors and trustees to pay any just debts, taxes, and expenses in winding up my estate." Whatever dreams and plans you make are meaningless unless you deal with this first clause in the will.

The first issue arising out of this first clause in the will is, how do you deal with the tax collector? What is the value of the underlying assets being transferred to the beneficiaries? Are these assets liquid assets, or are they shares in the family business or some other business in which you have a major stake?

In essence, the tax department has a first mortgage against the assets. Secondly, if there are personal guarantees to banks or lending institutions, there is a creditor that stands ahead of the family and other beneficiaries. So the issue of dealing with the obligations created under the first clause in the will is of utmost importance.

Since the underlying values of the business and other assets may be changing rapidly, it is necessary to review the cash needs of the estate on a regular basis. No one has created a more certain or economic way of dealing with cash at death than through the use of life insurance.

Let us assume that one has adequately planned to deal with the first clause in the will and has provided the cash necessary to pay the taxes, any guarantees to the bank and to provide for any other expenses in settling the estate. What then is the next issue?

The next issue is, how does the widow and family receive income? A second part of this same issue is, "Can the source of the income be secure and independent of the business?" If you ask a businessman or business owner, "How important is this?" The answer you invariably get is, "Very, very important!" Where a business is involved, the usual structure is that all income is earned by the business, so the issue is, how can you separate that very important income to the family from the ongoing risks of the business?

If we review what is happening with the process so far, we see that when a man dies, the first call on his estate is the tax collector and other creditors. The second entitlement, because of the way the assets are usually structured, is the company or family business. The third and last to have rights are the widow and family.

Let's just think about this for a moment. If we had asked the business owner during his lifetime what his priorities were, he would probably have said, "My wife and family first, my company second, and last (or probably not even mentioned), the tax department and creditors." So here we have an incredible conflict that exists in most business owners' planning. The real situation is in exact reverse to what the business owner wants from his estate planning.

Let's say it again. The business owner's top priority is to have a secure and independent income for his wife and family; secondly, he wants his company to survive and prosper, and thirdly, he could care less about the tax department (yet he may feel some obligation to his creditors). In actual fact, these priorities develop in reverse order. The reality is that the tax department and creditors are first, the business is second and the family is last. If you ask him, "Is this what you want?" the answer is always a resounding "NO!"

Therefore, one simple objective of planning for the business owner can be to realign these objectives, and to make sure that the planning gives the business owner the comfort that the real plan will deal with the real issues in the right priority.

Conceptually there is nothing complicated about this. Once the decision has been made, everything else is just details. Now the technicians can proceed to put the important details together such as tax planning, estate freezes, trusts, insurance, etc. Unfortunately the business owner too often is involved in these technical issues before having made a clear decision on the objective or without defining the priorities.

Assuming that provisions are made for sufficient cash in the estate to deal with the first clause in the will as well as providing for a secure, independent source of income to the widow and family; what, then, is the third or next important planning point? I believe it is to deal fairly with the children.

This may sound simple, but it may be the most complicated part of the whole exercise. If there is no family business involved, then "fairly" might mean the equal distribution of the family assets to the children on the death of both parents. That sounds simple and straightforward. However, if there is ongoing management of the assets required, then it is important to designate who among the children will manage the assets. This is critical if there is a family business involved.

On the death of the business owner, and where there is a family business involved, it is very important that there be a designated successor. In some cases it can work if the successor is the surviving spouse. Usually, one or more of the children are involved in the business, and the parents should make a decision while they are still around as to who will have the authority to run the business. What we are talking about here is the succession plan.

Since family businesses form the largest percentage of active, successful businesses in our society, let's deal with this issue. If you sit with mother and father and discuss their family business and how they want it handled on the death of the last survivor, mother will tell you that she wants it to be equal. This is a very natural feeling on the part of the mother, as she wants each of her children to be treated equally, and considers that to be fair. But is it? Mother is not usually actively working the business, so this seems to be the right answer to her. But father, who is working in the business, knows how difficult it is on a day-to-day basis to be successful, to fight off the competition and to make all the decisions every day that will help the business succeed and prosper.

If one of the children is already working in the business and has shouldered some of that responsibility, it is the father's inclination to say, "I want to be fair to the kids. I want Johnny, who is already in the business, to have a much stronger position than his siblings, possibly even control." If that turns out to be the game plan, then Johnny should be given a larger share of the business on the death of the parents and equality can be created by leaving other assets (real estate, cash, insurance proceeds, etc.) to the other siblings.

This area of succession planning has caused devastation among many family businesses. The first problem is when the founder doesn't make a decision and leaves control of the family enterprise to his executors with no clear set of instructions as to who the successor is to be. A classic case comes to mind where a very successful business owner, Mr. S, had built a strong wholesale business over the years. By the end of the 1980s his company was worth $3.5 billion and employed approximately 3,000 people. Unfortunately Mr. S was also very secretive, which is often part of the make up of these highly successful entrepreneurs. In the early 1990s he died. The family was not able to agree on a course of action and the siblings started legal action to gain control of the company. There were two daughters, one of whom was married to an executive in the business who had a very strong potential to be the successful leader and successor. But the family fighting got into the courts, and after five years this great enterprise declared bankruptcy. The crucial problem was the secrecy of the founder and the fact that he was not willing to put the problems on the table and talk them out with his family and his senior executives while he was still around.

Now, there is another situation with one of my clients where the founder decided twenty years ago to select his successor from among his four children. He selected his youngest son Bill. At the time he made this decision he also decided to change the share capital of the company, giving all the growth shares to his four children, including Bill.

Bill has run the company very successfully. He also had great faith in its future and has used some of his personal funds to buy additional shares for himself. The shares that the siblings acquired were all new shares with no value. Because of the success of the company, they each have realised phenomenal gains with each of the children now having in excess of $5 million in share value.

Bill has done a great job. His parents are delighted with his performance and dedication. So this story should have a happy ending, shouldn't it? Well that's not quite the case. For several years the other three siblings have been very jealous of Bill and quite critical of the perks he enjoys as president of the company. They also resent the fact that since Bill has bought additional shares, his worth is substantially greater than each of theirs. In fact, although they have no interest in either the company or its progress, they have each decided they would like to get cash for their shares and as much cash as the market will bear.

This has made Bill's life miserable and the siblings have added to his misery by hiring a lawyer to deal with their brother. It is hard to know whether this could have been avoided, or how it may have been avoided, but there is an excellent point to be made for stronger family communication.

At the time that the share structure was changed, if the founder had called his four children together and had discussed how important it was for them to work together, or if they had been allowed the opportunity to express their views and adopt a family approach to the problem (which would have also satisfied the needs of the business), things may have worked out differently. It doesn't always work out, but such family councils add greatly to the possibility that whatever plan is decided upon will be more successful.

It is important that the family have the kind of discussion that not only deals with the issue of equality, but also deals with the issue of fairness. Family meetings should be encouraged. It is much better to discuss these issues while changes can still be made. When Mr. Business Owner dies, it's too late.

Another part of this is to consider the future of the business and how important it is that the planning support that future and the possibility that the business can be carried on successfully. If several siblings who are not active in the business are involved, it may be necessary for Bill, who is running the business, to severely impair the business's viability by having to buy out the siblings at some point. This should be avoided at all costs.

One of the main reasons for the success of family businesses is the fact that they have patient capital. Usually companies are passed down from one generation to the other without having to withdraw capital to pay out shareholders. A very undesirable consequence of not planning carefully in this area is that companies start trading in their own shares. This also must be avoided at all costs.

As far as the children themselves go, ownership in the business should be considered a privilege and not a right. Usually quick solutions to these problems tend to be a disaster. These problems are complicated and require a good deal of thought. The important thing is to get a process of planning in place, which has the parties discussing the various options and getting to understand what fairness means.

The next principal issue is, how does the business owner provide that his estate planning is such that he leaves a financially healthy business? Therefore, in addition to making sure that there is a successor in place who will have a good degree of competence and experience to carry on the business successfully, it is important to make sure that the business is well financed. This is another reason why the business owner should make sure there is enough cash in his estate to pay the taxes on his death and to pay the guarantees to the banks. It is so that the cash drain on the business will be minimal. It was Oscar Wilde who once said, "Money says more in a moment than the most eloquent lover can say in a lifetime."

When the business owner dies, it is important that the company have sufficient capital to carry on successfully, even if the successor makes a mistake or two. Therefore, the company needs a long-term, viable strategic plan.

The next important issue to consider in estate planning is that the business owner should try to arrange a retirement income plan that allows him to transfer control to a successor during his lifetime and still have an adequate income, independent of the business. This will give the business owner a greater incentive to transfer control during his lifetime. If this transaction is successful, the business owner will have the joy of seeing his successor continue to develop the business in a dynamic way as the successor is bringing in new and younger ideas. This whole process means that the business has a greater chance of continuing and remaining competitive. It also allows the business owner to retire and continue to act as a mentor to the successor. This should be done on the basis of being available if the successor requires some advice. It is extremely important that once the business owner has transferred control, he should recognise that he must let the successor really run the enterprise. The most successful and dynamic companies are those that change leadership before they fall behind in these rapidly changing times.

In summary, if you want to demystify the estate planning process, you should really look at five major planning objectives. Most of these objectives involve making sure that there is sufficient cash available to finance the estate. Again, life insurance is the most certain and economical source of cash at death.

1. The first is an examination of the will and provision to deal with the first clause in the will by ensuring there are sufficient funds to pay taxes, creditors, etc.
2. The second main issue is to make sure there is an independent source of income for the widow and family.

3. The third is to treat the distribution of assets to the children fairly.

4. The fourth is to make sure that the business can continue as a financially healthy enterprise.

5. The fifth is to create an independent source of retirement income so that the business owner can step aside during his lifetime and transfer control of the enterprise to his successor, if that is the best option.

These various issues are independent of estate freezing techniques, tax planning issues and all those technical details which, important as they are, are not understood for the most part by the business owner.

The issues and the objectives we have been talking about are in areas where the business owner not only understands, but can also probably provide the most effective answers. After all, he has been used to dealing with the complications of running a business in our competitive society, so he must be one of the best decision makers in society. And if he knows the right questions, he can make good decisions. We can help by asking him those key questions.

Rehearse Great Meetings

Most often the process of developing a client requires several interviews. Quite often I will have a very brief agenda for the second meeting. This agenda is developed through a discussion with either my associate on the case or my technical backup; in essence, whoever is associated in dealing with the case with me, whether it is an active partner involved in the marketing or a member of our technical staff.

This rehearsal is extremely important, because what we want to accomplish is to prepare the items on the agenda based on a discussion of my first interview with the client. The rehearsal helps us go over all the main issues and talk about what questions are likely to come up. I should point out that a detailed report of each interview is always kept in the case file.

In a discussion of a half hour to an hour, we should be able to structure the agenda, discuss each of the main points, review the issues and discuss which questions are likely to come up. By going through this careful preparation with members of my team, it is likely that I am having a discussion with someone who is going to be far tougher than the client.

The rehearsal also helps me feel prepared and confident that there are not likely to be any issues raised by the client that we haven't already discussed and are prepared for.

The agenda may look something like this:

1. Have the client describe what took place in the first interview.
2. Try to help him define his set of objectives.
3. Take each of these objectives and ask questions so that they can be developed in some depth.
4. Ask him to prioritize the objectives.
5. Discuss alternative options or solutions for each of the objectives.

The first item on the agenda, asking him to relate what happened at the first meeting, is very important. Usually he will tell you what is really important to him. That is far more valuable than your relating what you thought the first meeting was about.

The second item on the agenda, defining the objectives, is a natural outflow from this discussion. Discussing and asking questions about each of the objectives helps both he and you to determine what is really important to him, and that leads naturally to the fourth item on the agenda, which is to prioritise these objectives. This sets up an action plan.

Having determined what objectives have priority, and having discussed some of the alternatives and options relative to those objectives, he will be asking for more specific information on how he can deal with getting to where he wants to go. This second interview may be the Action Interview, and so a third meeting may not be necessary. However, if a third meeting is necessary, then we go through the same procedure of setting up the agenda. Once again, I meet with my associate(s) and have a rehearsal discussion and preparation for that third meeting.

A likely agenda for the third meeting may be as follows:

1. A review of the objectives and their priorities.

2. Which of these objectives is a jugular versus a capillary item?

3. Alternative courses of action for dealing with the jugular items.

4. The clients choice of the best alternatives for dealing with each of these jugular items.

5. What is the next step with respect to each of these jugular items?

6. At what point would he like to deal with the capillary issues, the issues that are not as important?

This third meeting is the Action Meeting. It is important that only the key jugular questions be resolved at this time. It is also very important to set aside the non-urgent issues for later action.

The client may not have an accurate understanding of the process and what all the issues are, but he does have very powerful antennae that tell him whether or not you are prepared. When you are prepared you deal with things in a far more confident way, and that in itself is a positive message. Being prepared doesn't mean having all the answers — it means understanding the key questions.

I cannot stress too strongly how valuable and how important it is to have these rehearsals, these case discussions.

Use Graphics

Someone once said that a single picture is worth a thousand words. In conveying concepts and ideas, one or two pages of graphics can tell a story that's easily understood. Let me give you a personal example of this.

Some time ago I was dealing with a client who was buying a substantial pension plan involving some life insurance, and I was having great difficulty in getting him to understand how the plan worked and what the benefits were. The plan had actually been arranged on his behalf by the board of directors of the company, and they had looked at all options, including paying some additional bonuses, etc. On careful examination of the tax consequences on each of the alternatives, it became apparent that the plan that was proposed gave him the best long-term answer.

However, once the plan was in place, he wasn't satisfied that this was the route he should go. We had provided him with pages of documentation to show how it all worked and how it made sense for him and how we had considered all the factors. However, none of it seemed to get the message across.

I then asked my technical associate to redesign the plan to come up with a graphic showing the pension amount produced by our proposal as a blue block and the pension amount produced by taking bonuses and paying the tax as a grey block. He developed a very simple graphic and we took it to the client. We walked into the client's office and I took out a very thick file representing all the discussions and all the information we had developed. I said to the client, "Bill, would you like me to go through all the detail or would you like me to go straight to the bottom line?" Bill gave the expected answer, "Straight to the bottom line." I then handed over the one page graphic, which clearly showed that the blue block was substantially better than the grey block. I then asked the simple question, "Bill, do you want the blue block or the grey block?" He studied it for a moment or two and then said to me, "Well, the blue block looks much better, but could you explain it to me?" I turned to my technical associate and said, "Mark, can you explain it to Bill?" After about a five-minute discussion focusing only on the graphic, Bill was satisfied and we proceeded to wind up all the plan details.

Often when we are dealing with corporate insurance, we like to use a graphic, which shows how the insurance may flow into a company, or trust and then out to pay the estate or necessary tax obligations.

A graphic is a pictorial way of presenting a proposal so that it can be more clearly understood. It is the modern way of communicating with clarity. It is our feeling that whenever we can tell the story with a graphic, we prefer to use that particular method.

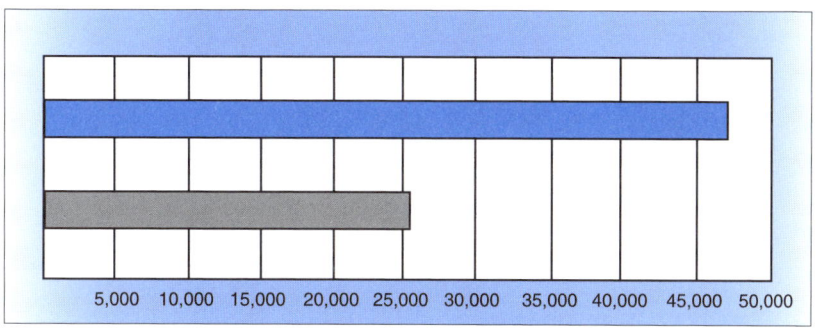

Sheltered vs. non-sheltered pension income:
After tax distribution comparison —
Sheltered (blue) vs. non-sheltered (grey) investment.

Dealing With The Business Owner

If we want to deal with business owners:

1. We need to know how businesses work.
2. We need to know the basics of business accounting.
3. We need to know the fundamentals of a corporation and a partnership.
4. We need to understand shareholder agreements and partnership agreements.
5. We need to know how businesses are taxed.
6. We need to know how the business markets its products and services.

These are the hard facts. They are usually technical details that are important to the process.

Now we will look at the soft facts, but you will have to put all this technical knowledge aside and recognize that the business owner is a human being with hopes, dreams, aspirations and concerns. Sometimes it's hard to avoid telling the business owner how much you know, but biting your tongue and listening will help the client.

The business owner may have several companies and a very complicated business, but that same owner usually has only one, legal family. That same business owner has only one valid estate plan and one valid will. In fact, his will is the only valid estate plan and also the last message that business owner will send to his family, his business partners, his employees and his community. How important is that message to him?

If I asked the question, "How important is that message to you?" the answer I get is always the same: "Very important!"

For many years I thought that "estate planning" cases were too complicated and beyond my ability to deal with. Then I made an amazing discovery. Most other insurance agents had this same feeling. What I believe we were all afraid of was the technical tax planning which was the venue of the specially trained tax technicians, lawyers and accountants. I made one other important discovery: that is, the clients also thought this technical tax planning process was too complicated — and they usually didn't understand it either.

Technicians are great at designing sophisticated tax solutions, but often they aren't as good at explaining these plans to the client. Some insurance agents have achieved a similar level of technical sophistication. The clients really don't want the technical details of these plans. For the most part they don't care what the tax plan and the insurance plan are. All they really want to know is what the plan will do for them.

So I learned that if I could find out enough about what the plan did or was supposed to do for the client, then I could become the client's interpreter. Once again, the key was to make no assumptions but rather to ask the right questions.

Another major problem in getting too sophisticated and complicated with the client is that people don't take the first step if they can't see where they're going. Just think of the last time you were out visiting and you left your home in the evening and there was a deep fog outside. How fast did you go down the stairs? Not very fast. You would feel your way fairly carefully for the first and second steps. The quickest way to get the client to act is to clear away the fog. That is why the concept of realigning priorities is so valuable. It gives the client a very simple road map.

In many cases the client never does take that first step, and a very large percentage of business owners die without a viable estate and succession plan in place. In respect to the general population, I estimate that something like fifty percent of business owners die without a will.

The business owner is not the only one that may be caught in that fog. Everyone around him assumes he has great advisors, and that because of the success of his business, he must have the good sense to have a viable estate and succession plan in place. They feel that a good business owner must have thought the issues through, and with the help of his very capable advisors has taken care of the strategic long-term plan for the business.

Here is what my good friend, Joe Dickstein, says about the role of the advisor, "A solution should represent the comfort level of the client and not the brilliance of the advisor."

It is very important to recognize that there are two key roles involved: the role of the planner and communicator and the role of the technician. I embrace the role of the planner and like to form a partnership with the technician, because both functions are vital to a successful planning process.

The solution should represent the comfort level of the client, not the brilliance of the advisor.

Telling a Story On Film — The Sturdy Family

One of the most exciting developments of the modern, high tech revolution is the opportunity to present a story on film.

For all life insurance agents, the ideal client would be a businessman who has had a severe heart attack, doesn't know whether he is going to survive or not, and is convalescing at the hospital with lots of time to think about what's happening with his business, his family and the community. Now, I don't wish this situation on anyone, but when it happens, the mindset of that person changes.

This businessman has now become acutely aware of the importance of his will, the importance of his family's future well being and the continued success of his business. This businessman can still change his will, he can still meet with his advisors and he can still make plans regarding the future management of his company. But the one thing he cannot do is to arrange for financing of payment of any taxes due on his death, the reduction of any debts or the provision of any capital to his company to help future management. He can't buy life insurance. He has all the worries and all the concerns, but very little ability to change the financial situation.

Now let's change this just a little bit. Let's assume that the heart attack has killed him. Let's also assume that, through some miracle, he was given a second chance and was brought back to life in good health with the ability to make some of the financial changes that are required. Do you think his awareness would be at a high level? What kind of discussion would he likely have with his family and advisors?

In reality you cannot do this. You cannot kill a client and then arrange for him to come back so that he can understand the importance of some of the planning issues that he should have dealt with while he was alive. But there is an opportunity for each of your clients to see a case history where this actually happens.

Through my association with CAFE (The Canadian Association of Family Enterprises), I was asked to prepare a course on Estate and Succession Planning. As its name suggests, CAFE is an organization across Canada of small, medium and large family-owned businesses. In fact, in Canada and the United States, family businesses account for about forty-five percent of the total economy.

When I was first asked to take on this assignment, I looked over all the material that I could find in North America that dealt with estate planning and succession issues. One of the items I studied was a video case history that had been prepared for CAFE several years before. The case history concerned a plumbing contractor who had been very successful over the years and had developed a business across Canada that, at the time of his death, employed five hundred workers.

The video is narrated by Alma Sturdy, the widow of Harold Sturdy, a successful plumbing contractor. It tells her story of having to make decisions about her four children, including

Brad, who was groomed as Harold's right-hand man and who had always made his career in the family company. Alma tells how Harold had his severe heart attack and that she knew he wasn't going to make it. When she was at his bedside for the final time Harold said to her, "Alma, whatever else you do, please be sure to treat the children fairly."

Alma goes on to talk about the dilemma this creates for her in the months after Harold's death and how she finally decides to divide the business equally among the four children.

Five years pass. Alma then relates the problems that developed over the course of those years: how Brad had to raise money to buy out two of his siblings and how the company had acquired considerable debt and eventually, how the business was lost. This segment closes with Brad asking the question, "Dad, is this fair?"

With this case history as the foundation, I decided to use this video as the basis for the course on Estate and Succession Planning.

I do the commentary in the video, and at one point, after Alma Sturdy tells her story, I say, "Wouldn't it be helpful if we could reconvene a meeting of Alma Sturdy, her son, Brad, the accountant, lawyer and insurance agent who participated in the original planning, and have them discuss what went wrong."

The next scene shows a boardroom with six chairs, and each of the participants is introduced and sits in their chair leaving one chair open. I then say, "Wouldn't it be great if we could bring Harold Sturdy back; if we could bring him back to life and have him sit in that sixth chair and discuss with his widow Alma and his son Brad and his three advisors what went wrong, and how they might do it better this time?"

This boardroom scene has been a powerful motivator for business owners throughout the world wherever this video has been shown.

In reviewing the material for this book, I came across my notes for the various participants when we planned the "boardroom scene". These participants were Harold Sturdy (the resurrected businessman), his wife Alma, his oldest son Brad, his accounting advisor Len, his legal advisor Diana, and his insurance advisor Pat.

In the boardroom scene Harold is talking about what happened when he first went about the planning.

Harold Let me tell you what happened as I remember it. I was in very good health. The business was going great. Brad was doing a good job and we spent a lot of time together talking about the business. Alma and I had some good holidays together, and when we were home it was hectic. I was spending all my time at the business. She was trying to help Debbie, Martina and Jeff get on with their lives. I assumed that I had lots of time to deal with the future of the business. I had no sense of urgency, and I didn't realise that I was just one heartbeat away from the destruction of my family and the business.

Alma We had a good life. I had my hands full dealing with Debbie, Martina and Jeff. I assumed Harold was looking after everything to do with the business. I knew he loved the kids and me. He talked about the business a lot. He was proud of how well Brad was working out. I assumed he had made plans to look after us — I should have asked some questions.

Brad Dad and I spent a lot of time together. He listened to my ideas on sales and advertising. He helped me to become part of the team. It was great! I was concerned about what would happen if Dad died, but when he met with the advisors Len, Diana and Pat, I wasn't included. I didn't feel I could talk to him about his death. I trusted him to look after the company and me. I should have found a way of talking to him.

Len Harold appointed me as an accountant when the first big expansion occurred and the company went national. I

Sense of urgency — just one heartbeat away from decisions you may never have the opportunity to make.

helped him upgrade the accounting and reporting systems. It was a big job and expensive. In the few years before he died I would meet with him once a year for lunch. He talked about how well Brad was doing. The subject of estate planning came up at one of these lunches. He said, "You know I bought some insurance to take care of Alma. With the business going so well, Brad should do OK and maybe Jeff will straighten out and become a part of it. I've made sure Alma will be OK and I trust her to look after the kids. Harold gave me the feeling that he didn't want to pursue this. He always kept our meetings short because he knew the meter was running.

Diana Harold was referred to me by one of the partners who handled all the company's legal work. I was just made partner in charge of the Wills and Trusts division. When Harold came in I thought we should take the time to know more about the family and the business. But he was quite clear about what he wanted me to do. He wanted a simple will leaving everything outright to his wife, Alma. He said that he "didn't want to rule from the grave." So I did what he asked. I judged he wasn't the kind of client who was a good listener — he was a hard-driving businessman.

Pat Well, Harold and I belong to the same golf course. We played together a few times. He knew the business I was in but he let me know that if he wanted to talk insurance, he would call me. He was a man of his word and he did call. He said he needed some life insurance and asked me to meet him in his office. I knew his business was going really well, so I was quite excited about the meeting.

When the meeting started he took charge immediately. He said, "Look, Pat, if I die in the next few years I want Alma to be secure, independent of the business. My son Brad is working in the business and I don't want him to have to worry about his mother."

Well, he seemed to know what he was doing, so I arranged the coverage for him. Harold arranged for me to call Diana in order to get an insurance trust set up.

Harold breaks in: Well, I guess I did something right.

Brad Dad, we should have talked.

Len We could have accomplished the same thing for Alma and had Brad end up controlling the company.

Diana This time I would like to know that there is a set of objectives, and when I draw your will, that it covers those objectives.

Pat How much insurance and who owns it has to come out of that set of objectives and how Diana draws the will.

Len If we take the time to do it right, we should end up with a plan that meets the objectives, but will also be tax efficient.

Harold How much should we try to accomplish today?

Diana If you, Alma and Brad can agree on the objectives today, ninety percent of the job will have been accomplished. Pat, Len and I can put the answers together so that we have some options.

Harold What about the cost?

Pat It seems to me that I am the only one that doesn't have a meter running. The insurance amounts are going to come out of the objectives, and there is considerable flexibility in the way you pay the premiums and what cash flow will be required.

Len Harold, you don't have the meter running until Diana has a new will in place. Our main function after you set the objectives is to keep the tax costs down. So whatever fees you pay are going to result in substantial long-term savings.

Diana It makes my job easier if the family has a plan that works for them and the business. The fees will be for drawing the will to accurately reflect these wishes and to draw any trust agreements required. Those fees are going to be a tiny fraction of the cost to the family and the business if it isn't done right — you probably realise that more than anyone. How much did it really cost Alma, the company and the kids last time?

Harold When I ask about costs I am just trying to be a good businessman. Your answers make sense, but I want you to recognise that we still have a business to run so make sure we are getting value.

Alma Can we keep this simple? Brad and I have had lots of opportunity to know what doesn't work.

Brad Dad, I never said much before, but this time I want to be treated as one of the main stakeholders. Why don't you, mom and I have a meeting to consider both the family objectives and the long term plan for the company?

Harold Sounds good. What do you all think of that as the next step?

Pat That's great, but I think we should spend a little more time today developing a short list of key objectives. Then Diana, Len and I will have something to work on. We should consider a time for the next meeting and keep the process going. In the meantime, Harold, you, Alma and Brad can have a family meeting and get the input of the other kids if you wish.

Harold I agree. Let's take a little more time today, and set the time of the next meeting. Let's be sure we've thought this out carefully this time, and that we're moving ahead to get it all done.

This video, *Winning the Succession Game*, is currently used as a teaching tool and as such is very entertaining while getting across a very strong message regarding estate planning.

It had always been my belief that the best way of communicating to a client what the problems would be on his death, would be to kill him with the provision that he could come back the next day and see how things were working out. However, there are severe penalties for homicide, so this didn't seem to be a very practical solution, especially since we do not yet know how to successfully resurrect a client.

But I decided that it would be incredibly valuable to business owners if I could create this situation on film, and have Harold Sturdy come back to meet with his wife, Alma and his son, Brad, who was now running the company along with the advisors. What we are really doing here is giving Harold Sturdy a second chance to get the planning right.

This planning meeting in the video takes place in a board room, and ten minutes of this board room scene was shown at the 1998 meeting at the Top of the Table at La Quinta, California. The dialogue is incredibly powerful and motivating, and the members of the Top of the Table who attended that session recognized what a strong vehicle this was, not only for business owners, but also for advisors who have to deal with estate and succession planning issues.

Currently this video is used as a teaching tool by CAFE for all its Canadian chapters. It is also being used by a number of universities in Canada. One of the major accounting firms has copies of the video in each of its offices across the country. This video has been shown at many tax and estate planning meetings and is an excellent vehicle to be used at trade associations. It has also been used widely as the main segment of a discussion on estate and succession planning.

Towards the end of the video I make this statement, "We and our clients will have to get it right the first time. This second chance that Harold Sturdy had was just a figment of our imagination. Showing it on film allows the viewers to get an idea of what kind of problems can develop and what the process has to be to deal with those problems."

This case history has a powerful influence on all viewers. Many business owners and advisors have been motivated to pay the professional fees and the insurance premiums to get the job done after seeing the video.

In summary, this video helps the viewer to have an awareness of the problem and also helps the viewer see the emotional and practical issues involved. It also shows the great cost of not thinking about and dealing with the problem. In the end, the client pays fees to lawyers, accountants and tax practitioners, and pays premiums to provide the insurance necessary to finance the plan. One cannot discount this cost, but it is not the main cost. The main cost is the time that the business owner needs to devote to the project. This cost is dealt with in a very practical and direct way during the boardroom scene when the Accountant says, "You either pay a little bit now to solve the problem, or a whole lot more later if you don't solve the problem."

Films and videos can be a great aid in marketing the services of all the professional advisors, and are of particular value to those of us in the life insurance industry. Utilizing the video is a little like the car salesman putting the prospective buyer behind the wheel and saying, "Take it for a drive and see how you feel about it." In this case the prospective client can take a look at the video, and it tells him almost all the things he needs to know to be able to consider the problem areas, the potential solutions and how the process works.

For information on ordering the video *Winning the Succession Game*, please see the last page of this book.

How Do You Handle Losing?

No matter how good we are and how great a presentation we've made, or how well we've listened to the client, or how effectively we've communicated the process, from time to time we are going to lose.

This should be looked on as a great positioning opportunity. The development of a successful business and a strong base of good clients is a long-term exercise. No matter what the prospective client tells you, he may have an obligation that rules you out as a supplier. In the worst case you may have said something which has offended him or put him off. We can't really know, in every case, what his reason is for choosing another supplier. The only thing we can do is to use this opportunity to convey a great message, and to make some lemonade. The key is to make sure you keep your door wide open.

What should that message be?

The first part of the message should be that you wish to congratulate him on solving the problem. That's his primary interest. Second is to show a willingness to co-operate with the other agent in any way that is useful to the client. I usually do this by way of a letter as soon as possible after I have heard the bad news. The purpose of this is obvious. Usually the client is concerned about having to say no and using another supplier, and the message I want to give him is that I think he has done the right thing in solving the problem, and that I am still there for him if he needs me. What I have done is positioned myself as the alternative supplier on any future transactions. I have left him with a good feeling about me and how I do business.

Let me give you an example. We were negotiating with a large company to provide insurance funding for a shareholders' agreement for Roy and Bill. We were brought into the case by their accountant, and had two very good meetings. However, before the transaction could be completed, they advised us that a good friend of Bill's had entered the life insurance business and they were going to transact the purchase of the new insurance through this new agent. In discussing this matter with our referral source, it became obvious that we had lost this case.

The first thing we did was to write a letter to both Roy and Bill personally, sending a copy to their accountant (our referral source). In essence what we said was that we wanted to congratulate them on dealing with the problem and getting their agreement funded; and that if there was anything we could do to assist the other agent regarding any material we have gathered to let us know. We also said that we would like to stay in contact, and that if we could be of any service in the future, we would be delighted to talk with them.

Well, about two weeks later the accountant called us, and he told quite an interesting story. He said that, prior to going into the insurance business, this new agent was Bill's son's athletic coach. Also, this new agent was getting married and Bill was to be the master of ceremonies. (It was obvious that the relationship was very strong.) He also told us that there had been another agent working on the account, and the other agent had also written a letter, but this letter had berated Roy and Bill because he too had met with them and felt that they should have done business with him.

The accountant then went on to tell us that Roy and Bill were very delighted with our letter, and that we were certainly still in their minds as a possible future supplier. The other agent had, of course, been written off.

Well there is a happy ending to this story. It so happened that the new agent got married, Bill was his master of ceremonies, and a few months later, the new agent was out of the insurance business. But the shareholder funding transaction had not been completed. Subsequently we were called in, and over a period of time handled all the funding and, of course, embarked on a very close relationship with Roy and Bill. Their company has been very successful and much more insurance has recently been purchased through our office.

The moral of the story is, "When you lose, do it with a touch of class, and position yourself to be the alternate supplier whenever the client determines they are going to do additional business." It is a matter of the supremacy of good business sense over negative emotions.

Don't misunderstand me. We fight in every way that we can to save an account, but when we lose, we recognize it, and it is our standard procedure to make lemonade out of this lemon.

How Do You Deal With The Gatekeeper?

I make a specific effort to build a relationship with the personal secretary or the chief executive assistant for my principal clients. It is important to recognize how powerful these executive assistants can be. My style in dealing with them is to utilize their talents at every opportunity.

I like to ask them if they will help me to schedule a meeting time that will be most beneficial to the client (their boss). I give them an indication in general terms of what I want to talk about, and how long it is going to take. By having this discussion and showing my confidence in them, they know I am making their job easier. They also know that I am recognizing that they have some power in terms of the schedule.

It is important to have an ally within the company. And sometimes, for me, this ally is the executive assistant. I always find some way of saying, "thank you" and recognizing their help. They are all on my Christmas list, and I make sure they are treated as VIPs.

Sometimes, someone who wants to get to their boss will treat this key member of the team carelessly, and even thoughtlessly. If you do this, you have just written off the account.

Let me give you a classic example. Grace is the executive assistant to a very shrewd businessman who owns a number of companies. One day I asked Grace whether she had any problem calls and how she dealt with them. She proceeded to tell me about the various kinds of suppliers' calls where they didn't recognize her position, and tried various forms of subterfuge to get to the boss. From what she said to me, it was clear that those suppliers were unlikely to get anywhere unless they dealt with her.

You see, what these suppliers didn't know is that for about the last six years, Grace had been married to the boss; and since it was his second marriage, it wasn't well publicized and she had kept her maiden name. One didn't have to have a vivid imagination to understand what happened to a supplier who tried to go around Grace.

Many of these assistants put up with issues of male chauvinism and pushy people who don't always recognize when somebody else is trying to do their job in a professional way. It is just another case of where people skills and relationships can be very helpful.

Does the 'Deal Killer' Really Exist?

Many years ago I remember working with John, a very capable insurance agent, who was having great difficulty getting sufficient volume. He dressed well. He worked hard. He made the calls, but he wasn't getting the results. One day he came into my office and was very dejected and asked if he could spend a few minutes with me discussing his problems.

I asked John to tell me about his problems, and he proceeded to relate a story about the last several interviews that he had. He indicated that he had developed a significant resentment for accountants. So I asked him why this was, and he proceeded to tell me that he had been quite successful in contacting businesses and getting meetings with the company accountant, but in most of these cases, nothing was happening. John had positioned himself at his comfort level, and his comfort level was to deal with employees rather than the business owner or shareholder.

After our discussion he had a choice; the choice was to bite the bullet and call the decision-maker. But he never got up the nerve to do this, and a month or two later he was out of the business.

Sometimes the business owner will use these senior employees to say no for him. Or he may use his outside advisor. This seldom happens if you go through the process of a broad concept interview where the business owner is dealing with his family and his business and his charities. These are non-technical issues that he can understand.

Now, if the business owner and I had been through that discussion and then he asked me to contact his accountant or one of his advisors, I am delighted to do so. Although, rather than my meeting with the advisor or senior employee, I usually have my associate, who does all my technical work, conduct that meeting. I often say to the client, "We've identified the issues that are important to you, and if you would like us to deal with the technical and tax issues, then I have an associate who can meet with your advisor and have that discussion."

Sometimes the client will say, "No, Hal, I would like you to meet with my advisors." I will then ask the client what he would like me to discuss. The client may say that his advisor has always been in the picture when he is making a decision of any importance, and that he would like his advisor to know what is going on.

I have to tell you that I don't get this request very often, but when I think back, I know it used to happen more often twenty years ago. Here is the way I would handle that meeting.

I ask the client to have the advisor call me so that I can arrange an appointment with him. This is important because I don't want to be chasing the advisor. I want the advisor to get specific instructions from the business owner. We then have the meeting and my first question is, "What would you like to know about my discussion with Mr. Business Owner?"

He usually says. "Well, he asked me to meet with you because he is contemplating taking out some insurance."

I say, "We haven't reached that stage yet, but when we do, I would like my associate, Mark, who handles the technical aspects of my business, to meet with you and get your advice on the tax and technical issues."

He says, "OK, but where is the discussion at this point?"

I say, "I think I can take you through the key discussion, and it goes something like this: Let's assume Mr. Business Owner died last night. The first clause in his will commits his executors to pay the costs of settling the estate and to pay any just debts and taxes. Do you know how much it would cost to clear that first clause in the will?"

The advisor says, "Well I really don't have a calculation, but I could put one together in respect of the taxes. I'm not sure about the other matter."

The second question I asked him is, "If Mr. Business Owner died last night, who will be running the business today? Do you have a feeling as to who that would be?" Another question I might ask is, "Who would that individual be reporting to?" In other words, who are the executors who have the authority?

The typical answer I get back from the advisor is that he is very pleased I am looking into this, that he is sure we can handle these questions, and to let him know what information we need from him and that he will be glad to help.

The fact is that he hasn't thought about these issues. He doesn't want this job, and he can't wait to hand the ball back to me and my staff.

I treat this meeting very carefully. Before I go to the meeting, I have an in-depth discussion with one of my associates to make sure I've discussed all the questions. The advisor will immediately sense whether you're prepared and confident. If you're not, he will take control — and maybe he should.

In the unlikely case that the advisor has a handle on everything, I am going to ask him questions, and really, we are right back to the process of defining what the key issues are, but this seldom happens. As I stated previously, in the vast majority of cases he can't wait to get rid of the problem. This client is important to him and he knows that he is stepping outside his field.

I seldom, if ever, make a proposal on the specific planning steps without a client defining or acknowledging the agenda and being prepared to go into those steps. Usually I utilize my staff to work with his advisors in dealing with tax and technical issues. My role is to manage the account and handle the people issues and relationships.

We have developed a team approach where each of the producers can call on back-up support to do the technical and tax work with the client's advisors. In that way I am dealing with the client at the level he understands. I am dealing with the overall game plan for his family and his business, and I leave it to my technicians to deal with his technical and tax advisors. In many cases I am not even present at those meetings with the client's advisors; but I am certainly ready if I am needed.

As Larry Wilson said in his great book *Changing the Game*, "We've reached a new stage in marketing that in many cases requires a team approach rather than transacting business as a lone ranger." He says that the process will be a vendor team meeting with a purchasing team to work out and engineer the best transaction for the benefit of the purchaser. This may be slower, but in the end will result in larger transactions.

At our office we have certainly found this to be the case, and strongly recommend the team of the technician to review documents, tax issues, etc., and the producer with the people skills, to get the best results for the client.

The Dream Merchants

As I mentioned before, from time to time people ask me what I do. I find this a great opportunity and usually say that I get paid by selling life insurance, but that is not what I do. So then, the next question is, "How do you explain that; what is it that you do?"

I respond by saying, "I am involved in a very specialized area of planning and it is very difficult to describe. However, it would be a lot easier for me to show you." This usually results in our setting up an appointment to talk about it, and the interview process begins.

That's what I say, but what I really feel is that we are in the business of "financing dreams."

All of us have our dreams. The business owner has dreams for the future of his family and his business, his community, the charities he supports and his favorite causes. When he meets with his advisors it is usually to set up trusts or an estate plan and will that sets out his wishes or dreams. A big part of our job is to ask questions and get involved in a reality check to find out if these wishes are actually financed. Now, let's go right back to the first clause in the will, which says, "pay the costs of settling my estate, pay my just debts and taxes." The dream here is that the family, the business and the charities will all benefit from the estate, but they can only benefit once the estate is cleared of its obligations. So, there is a price tag for financing that first clause in the will.

Let's assume the price tag is one million dollars. Let's also assume that there was no such option as life insurance. To satisfy that first clause in the will it is obvious that some assets would have to be sacrificed or the dreams will crash.

But there is life insurance, and if this business owner can qualify medically for life insurance, he can create a miracle. He can pay a few hundred dollars a year or a few hundred dollars a month, and create one million dollars of capital, tax-free. In effect, he pays interest (at a fraction of the cost of borrowing) and he creates capital. If the one million dollars is permanent coverage, then the premium required isn't the cost … it's an investment.

We have come to accept this miracle as an ordinary event. Let me give you an analogy. From time to time my wife Nancy and I have traveled to Europe, and periodically, on the flight back, I reflect on the fact that a journey that has taken me less than half a day took my father several weeks in traveling from Riga in Latvia to North America. As I fly smoothly along at six hundred miles an hour, I am in awe of the creative power of man that has designed this jet aircraft, which has changed our lives, and yet we take this wonderful change in our lives for granted.

But no less awesome is the accomplishment of the life insurance industry in creating a financial instrument that can allow a young man of 40 to buy one million dollars of insurance, which coverage he can either rent or own, depending on his situation. In most cases it will take a lifetime of earning and paying tax and saving to accumulate an estate of one million dollars.

There are many options in financial planning, many products and services, but our value is at its highest when we bring our people skills and knowledge and the miracle of life insurance to the table to create values for our clients, families, businesses, communities and charitable institutions.

When we deal with the "soft facts" of feelings, emotions and wishes, we are able to help people make their dreams a reality. Yes, life insurance is a miracle, and we are the "dream merchants." We show our clients how to financially underwrite their dreams!

The Best Questions

Earlier I mentioned the Chinese proverb that says, "Tell them and they may forget. Show them and they may remember. Involve them and they will understand." The world is full of answers. The problem for the process manager is to formulate the right questions so that the necessary answers become apparent to everyone concerned. It is by means of posing probing questions that the discovery stage of the process will be successful. A key objective of asking questions is to involve the client in the process.

1. What does your will say?

The question "What does your will say?" is a really productive way of turning the interview in a direction that flags problems and indicates the degree of thought and planning that the testator has invested in the process. As I have previously stated, the will is the only valid estate plan. This discussion leads naturally into several other key questions. If you are dealing with a business owner and there is no reference in the will to the business, it opens up a whole area of discussion as to the future of the business, succession, etc.

2. What does the first clause in your will say?

This is a great question for starting a discussion about the costs of clearing the estate. If you can visualize the stake holders sitting around a table, who would they be? The executors, widow and family would be one set, the creditors would be another set, and the tax collector would be a third set. The first issue is how much cash is needed to clear the table for the family. The second issue is how much cash and income will the family have independent of the business? (Remember that first clause directs the executors to pay the costs of settling the estate, pay the debts, and pay the taxes.) Your job is to ask how this will happen.

3. How do your executors get the cash to clear the estate?

Executors have found that estates may have too much real estate, too much in shares of private companies, but they never find an estate with too much cash.

There are only four sources of cash:

1. Existing cash.

2. Borrowing the cash.

3. Selling assets, and

4. Purchasing life insurance.

One has to be careful with the option of using existing cash. If it is in a corporation then what is the tax cost of getting the money out? In any event one should check the alternative cost of using life insurance. Even if liquidity is not a factor, economics may dictate that using the discount method of providing that cash through life insurance makes good business sense.

Borrowing the cash is always a last resort method. What if the loan is not available at the time it is required? What will the interest rate be on the loan? Let's assume that interest rate is a modest seven percent. Then a one million dollar loan would require annual interest payments of seventy thousand dollars. How will the capital be repaid? Life insurance may require an investment of two percent or three percent a year, and that buys the capital. There is no capital to be repaid.

Selling assets is a tough option. I always like the client to list his assets and then tell me which assets could be sold to raise cash.

I remember a discussion with a client named Larry. He quite proudly listed the various assets he had. Following is Larry's list:

LARRY'S LIST

Value of home	$1,500,000
Pension plan	$600,000
Cash and short term investments	$100,000
Shares in real estate development company	$5,000,000
Shares in a publicly traded computer company	$200,000
Apartment building	$2,000,000

So I asked Larry, "Which assets would you like to sell?" He had already told me that he would like his estate to have about two to three million in cash, so he started reviewing his list and said, "Well I wouldn't want to sell the house because my wife loves the house."

I said, "What about the pension?" and he said, "No, I can't sell the pension plan or cash in the pension plan, there would be too much tax to pay, and further, that goes to my wife tax-free."

So I said, "Well what about the shares in the development company?" And he said, "Well without me there I don't know what kind of price we would get for the shares in the short run, and it might take some time to dispose of those shares. I don't think that's the answer."

I then said, "Well then, what about the apartment block?"

"Actually that's producing good income and some of it is tax sheltered," he replied. "It's the one that would be the easiest to sell, but I wouldn't want my family to dispose of that asset."

I said to him, "What about the computer company? It's not very much but at least you would raise some cash." And he said, "Look, that's one of the best investments I have ever made. There is a great team running that company. I bought those shares for $20,000 just two years ago. No I wouldn't want them to sell those. They should hang on to those shares."

Then Larry asked, "Hal, how much did you say the insurance would cost?"

When you are examining selling assets as an option, it's important to get to the list of assets and discuss it. There are always costs. There are tax costs, commissions, fees, discounts, and the end result is usually a substantial discount over the real value. But the life insurance option creates full value for a discounted investment — it usually turns out to be the most attractive option.

When you ask what assets the estate would sell, you always get the same answer. The estate would have to sell the best assets and the family would be left with the dogs. "Is that what you want?" you ask, and the answer is always a resounding "No!" Then you examine the costs of selling assets. The end result is a substantial discount over value. Life insurance creates all of the value for a discounted investment.

The role of the professional advisor is to help the client eliminate uncertainty. Nowhere is that more evident than in the life insurance transaction. One of the least understood facets of this transaction is that the benefits occur when a valued loved one, often the head of the business dies. There is usually a period (often a long period) when the beneficiaries are consumed by grief. This is not a time for those same beneficiaries to be making important decisions.

Ideally, decisions involving money or the business should be delayed until such time as the beneficiaries are over the critical period of grief and are able to function in a normal way. In fact a well designed estate plan will recognize this and have safeguards in place to deal with important decisions and remove the immediate anxiety of financial matters. This failure to recognize the paralyzing effect of grief is a major source of problems for beneficiaries and executors. The cash provided by life insurance is a certain and simple way of alleviating those problems.

4. How much income do you want your wife and family to have?

This question is often accompanied by a qualifying statement: "independent of the business." I had a classic case that reminds me of how important it is to have retirement income or income being generated to a widow "independent of the business."

I had two clients, Joe and Mary, who in their late sixties decided they would retire and transfer their business to their two sons. At the time this decision was made they talked to their lawyers and accountants and came up with a plan to reorganize their business so that they would hold approximately two million dollars of preferred shares. These shares had the voting control in the company but all future growth would go to the two boys. They felt quite secure that they had reasonable pension plans. They received modest dividends from the preferred shares and the company owned the building, which had a value almost equivalent to Joe and Mary's shareholdings and also provided underlying security.

A few years went by and Joe died. Mary was still receiving her pension plan income plus dividends on her preferred shares. However, it wasn't too much later when the company started having financial difficulties. The sons had negotiated what they thought was a very attractive government contract, but it turned out that the margins were very low. Their accounts were slow to get paid and they had made some major changes to accommodate this account.

To make a long story short, the company was put into bankruptcy and Mary's two million dollars of preferred shares became worthless. Now, even though she has the controlling vote with the preferred shares, she had entrusted the day to day operations to her sons as her husband had done before her. The voting rights she had were of no help in the bankruptcy situation.

Unfortunately there are many situations where a class of shares is used to provide a widow's benefit or to provide a retirement benefit to the business owner. Maybe one should step back and say, "Would you ever put all your resources with a life insurance company that had a value of two million, five million or ten million dollars?" Yet that's what these individuals were doing by investing in their own company.

How secure is an investment in a company where the business owner has just died or retired? The discussion in the five-minute Coffee Interview in a previous chapter is a good example of the issues. In asking these questions it is important to remember that people think about these things, but they seldom put a plan in place that deals with the security problem. To the extent that you ask the question and focus on the problem you are providing a valuable service to your client.

5. *How much capital is required to provide that income?*

Again in the Coffee Interview, I dealt with the issue of how to determine the capital that is needed. It's important to deal with this carefully. The answer is basic to a sound plan.

6. *How important is it that your family is guaranteed that income?*

This is one of the most important questions to ask. I repeat this question for emphasis. "How important is it that your family is guaranteed that income?" This is a soft fact question. It's a question of feelings and attitudes. It gives your client the opportunity to consider his priorities. It's a critical point in his decision-making process. This should be handled very slowly and carefully. It is a key point in the interview.

7. If you had died last night, who is running the company today?

Sometimes it is necessary to deal with a critical point early in the discussion in order to focus attention on the importance of planning. Few questions are as effective as this one. If the company is one of the major assets, there needs to be a clear, well thought out plan for the business and how it is going to operate the day after the client dies. I remember having a meeting with a businessman and his wife, and when I asked this question he said, "No problem. My wife Mary knows the business and she could step in."

Well, not so fast. His wife immediately said that she didn't want to be involved in any way if her husband died! Whenever this question comes up I say, "Let's talk about it. Have you asked your wife (or son, or other family member) if she (or he) wants to run the business?"

Sometimes he'll say, "Oh my manager can run the business." So my next question(s) will be, "And who will he be reporting to? Is there any special reason that he will stay? Do you have some plan worked out with him? Is it documented?"

8. If you had died last night, are there taxes to be paid?

How would this be handled? Who will deal with it? Where will the cash come from? How can you clear the estate without dealing with this question? An estate may have too much real estate, too much of an investment in private company shares, but it will never have too much cash. The key provisions of an income to the widow and family may not work if an answer to this question cannot be found.

9. If you had died last night, how is the company's financial position today?

Someone once said every generation should try and leave the company in a better position for the next generation. Will that happen to your company?

10. The first clause in your will says, "Pay the expenses of settling the estate, pay the debts, pay the taxes." So the creditors and tax collector come first and the business and the family come last. Is that what you want?

The answer to this question is always a resounding, "No!" which helps to prove that the objective of estate planning is clearly to re-align the positions of the stakeholders and have the business and the family come first.

11. There are three main stakeholders in your estate:

    i) Creditors and tax collector.

    ii) Business.

    iii) Family.

Would you like to rearrange the priorities to these?

    i) Family.

    ii) Business.

    iii) Creditors and tax collector.

This is a motherhood issue but sometimes just reviewing the

process triggers the necessary interest and action.

12. What is the value of fifty percent or less of the shares of a private company?

This is where you end up will all the disadvantages of having property without any of the advantages. With fifty percent or less you can't make a decision without the support of another shareholder; however, owning the shares does subject you to tax, including death taxes. It is sometimes referred to as a great asset to have as a liability!

It is critical in this situation to have an exit strategy first. First, in event of death there should be an insurance-funded buy-sell agreement. Secondly, there should be an exit strategy in the event of disability, retirement, or dispute.

13. Have you co-signed your business's credit line?

Medium sized businesses and contractors often have to obtain bonding. They also have to deal with the bank. The business owners often forget that they have to sign personally for the companies credit line or bond. Since one of the key objectives to leave the company in good health when it passes to the next generation or to the estate, it's important to ask the question: "Have you signed twice for the company's line of credit?"

14. If you had died last night, what would the company's bank manager want to know today?

It's an important part of business insurance to cover off the risk. "If you had died last night, what would the company's bank manager want to know today?" I like to deal with this question by role-playing. I say, "If you had died last night and the bank manager calls this afternoon who would he want to speak to and what questions will he ask?"

15. What would you like to put on the agenda?

This is a particularly good question when you're confirming the second meeting. I have had some amazing responses to that question including the client telling me that "We really want to get insurance on our older partner. Let's make sure we get a medical organized for him," or "We think Jim's very important to the organization. We need to talk about additional insurance on him." It's like you're getting a preview of the actual meeting.

16. What are your main concerns?

This is a direction-setting question. It's the same thing as saying, "A penny for your thoughts." It is also a test of how comfortable the client feels with you. In essence you are giving him an opportunity to set the agenda, and that is an ideal starting position. It is also a great question to ask when you are well into the discussions. You may get some very important feedback.

17. How did you get started in the business?

This is a great question to use once you've established rapport. Most businessmen are lonely — there are many aspects of the business they would be afraid to discuss with their family or employees, but it's great for them to have a very interested listener who is there to help them. They love to talk about the business, and the answer to this question can take twenty minutes to half an hour. And while they are educating you on how far they've come and the problems they've handled, they are also reminding themselves. Your response should be to listen carefully and to ask relevant questions. This is a wonderful opportunity to bond with the client and establish a high level of comfort.

18. When you look five years ahead, what do you see for the business?

Once he has recited where he's been, a very good question can be, where do you see the business five years from now? This is the opportunity for him to tell you his dreams. He may tell you he has a son or daughter who's very interested in running the company. Maybe they are at college and work for the company in the summer. Maybe he tells you he's grooming a great manager and expects to take more time off and improve his golf game. Maybe he says he'd like to have a retirement plan in place by that time. No matter what he tells you, again it helps you to understand his agenda.

19. Questions relating to human life value.

What was the last critical decision this company had to make? Who was at that meeting? Before that, what was the last important decision? Who was at that meeting?

Questions relating to human life value help you to focus in on the decision makers and their value and importance to the company.

20. What's the next step?

This is a soft way of getting action. It is said when everything else has been said. It is not really a closing question because if the interview has patiently developed the issues, there is no need to be concerned about an identifiable moment in the process that is described as the close. The key is to convert discussions and concepts into a course of action. At this point I'll discuss the procedures for completing the transaction or the first step of the transaction. I usually follow up with a letter laying out the planning that needs to be done.

Know Your Business

When I decided to leave the comfort of being an agent employee in a branch some twenty years ago, it was a tough decision. The company paid the rent, hired the staff and administered every detail of my business. It was hard to walk away from all of that, but times were changing. I didn't understand all the changes but a few were becoming obvious. With the rapid changes in new money products, universal life and a higher demand for annuities and money products, it became obvious I had to be not only a supplier of services but also a purchaser for my clients.

The world is changing at an incredibly fast pace. The computer has given us the ability to design product, to illustrate with varying assumptions and to show graphically how a proposal would work. My knowledge was about a world that was fast disappearing. I realized that I had to position myself to deal with the new world that was emerging — but there was no way of understanding what that new world would be.

I believe that relationships and building long-term relationships will continue to be the key to success. I knew I wanted to control my own destiny. Rapid changes mean that we have to be able to react with speed to market conditions. These market conditions were changing in a revolutionary way. Fortunately great changes create great opportunity, although it can be very frightening to live through that change.

I had some decisions to make. I knew what I was leaving and I had to design what I wanted to replace it with. Fortunately I had a proven marketing plan that helped me to build loyal, long-term clients. Over seventy percent of my new business was with existing clients. The new style of operation would be as part of a team. I was creating a new and valuable role for myself. I wanted more in the way of a competitive edge. I wanted to deliver the best advice based on having excellent technical support — this had to both be the best and perceived as the best. I had already made a good start by having an association with a top technician I had helped train.

We were a good team. I managed the relationship and he provided the technical support. My dream was to develop a production line that could compete with anyone no matter what resources they had and how big they were.

"Tell them and they may forget. Show them and they may remember. Involve them and they will understand." Without my consciously realizing it, this old Chinese proverb became my philosophy of doing business as my organization grew and developed. I involved everyone in the dream. Our motto became: "Advice is only as good as the people you ask."

WE HIRE ATTITUDE! People can gain experience — they can develop skills — but attitude is the key. Everyone had to buy into the concept that excellence is a journey, a journey that can produce great rewards and a sense of fulfillment.

We asked our associates to buy into the dream and to be patient. We asked them to be team players and not lone rangers.

We believed that we all have to change and to share our talents. Today a very large part of our transactions involve more than one associate. Joint cases are the norm. We do the things that have to be done to get the best job done for the client. We partner with our suppliers and our referral sources.

We went into the professional community. We built bridges by providing information. We suggested that Zlotnik, Lamb & Company would be their technical resource for all information on insurance-based estate plans. We brought seminars to their offices and hosted a retreat once a year for tax practitioners. We told our referral sources we were there for them as an out of house resource with no pressure to refer business. We produced two quarterly papers — *Succession* and *The Retirement Income Report*. We wanted to have wide name recognition, so we advertised on a regular basis in the community's main newspapers. This was very successful and gave us a great profile in the local market. If there was a business function or a charitable project we were there. We sponsored and ran our own golf tournament, which has raised large amounts of money for key charities.

We could not have accomplished all this as lone rangers. In 1983 Peter Lamb joined me as a partner. Since then we have grown from a small office to one with around forty associates and staff. It wasn't easy, but we always worked toward our dream of being the best we could be at delivering the best answer for the client.

We have invested in our business, and we have spent a significant part of our income on promoting our image and our name.

We know that trust is the most valuable commodity we have to sell. We promise less and deliver more. We believe that being trustworthy is more than honesty and integrity. Those are the givens, but there is another key element and that is competence. In our marketplace we have made sure that we are referable. We have done everything possible to earn the right to referrals by having technical competence in every area of our market.

The bottom line of everything we do is to assign the best people to get the best job done for the client. For example, when a group specialist is appropriately needed, the job is handed over to our group department. All of our associates recognize that getting a share of more business and having a better job done for our client means that everybody wins. When our client's interest is served, it serves us all.

Therefore, in summary:

1. Position for name recognition.

2. Develop a target market.

3. Study every aspect of your offering.

4. Develop a series of questions that focus on the process rather than the transaction.

5. Patiently develop the buyer's understanding of the problems he is interested in solving.

6. Remember that creative problem solving arises out of in depth examination of the problems.

7. Recognize that the answer has to be far more important to the purchaser than the vendor. Remember that there is no such thing as the right answer. There are choices. The key is to pick the best of the alternatives the vendor needs to provide creative alternatives.

8. Questions are more important than answers. The service provider's success depends on his client's success.

9. Be trustworthy. This means more than honesty and integrity. A vital ingredient is competence.

10. Before going into a meeting go through a rehearsal of the issues; the buyer will know.

11. Ask the purchaser about his agenda. Always work to his agenda.

12. Learn to relax.

13. Deal with your fears.

14. Have fun.

Summing Up

This book talks about the importance of attitude — the importance of making lemonade out of lemons. Life is not easy, and all of us have to contend with disappointment and sometimes what appears to be defeat.

When we feel defeated we're dealing with negative emotions. Sometimes we react as victims, and allow ourselves to feel like losers. Maybe this happens to all of us at some point in our lives. This allows the lemon to sour us, to destroy or weaken our resolve. It gives credence to the idea that some external force can rule our lives. Maybe this is true, but at the age of 77 and after 55 years in a business I never intended to get into, I can't buy that idea.

Maybe the reason I feel that we have far more control over our destiny is the fact that the life insurance business gives us the maximum opportunity to make choices and to decide our own fate. Let me give a simple example. One of the more difficult things we do is phone for an appointment. I have heard many talks showing how if we say the right words in the right way we increase your success ratio, but that's not what my experience has been. I have found that if, before I picked up the phone, I thought carefully about the potential benefit to the client and the fact that the worst case for me was that I would have to find another name to telephone, my attitude would be positive. After reflecting on this for a few minutes, I make the call, and somehow, what I say communicates a sense of importance so that I am usually granted the interview.

Most people have incredibly sensitive antennae and can feel your mood, whether you're confident or tentative; whether you're nervous or relaxed — they don't concentrate on what you say, but on how you say it.

This is why I talk about rehearsing meetings with associates before going out to do the real thing. The fact is that every interview is a performance, and in the insurance business or estate planning marketplace, we can be paid many thousands of dollars for this performance. How prepared do you want to be? It's a given that we are knowledgeable and good at people relationships, but that isn't enough — it's critical to deal with the soft facts ... how people feel ... how people make decisions.

Unlike other professional advisors, we don't have a meter running. We work on contingency. The insurer pays us a commission if we're successful in helping the client find the solution to his problem.

Some agents feel they want to charge a fee for their services, and so be it. However, the rewards are high when we win, so I don't want to put any impediments in the way of starting the process of developing a potential client. The fact that there is no meter running is one of the great advantages we have. We can take the time to patiently develop the client's understanding by asking soft fact questions about his or her feelings and attitudes. It's very difficult for fee-based advisers to do this.

Our principal role in the Broad Concept Approach is to be the relationship manager. This puts us in the role of managing the process. We help with the most important issue, the diagnosis. Patience is a very important part of this process. The key element is to ask questions that help the client to see and understand his or her problems and to work together to define and prioritize the solutions. Ideally the client should share the excitement of discovering the most effective solution. Then we review all the options to make sure that the most certain and economic way of solving the problem is clearly understood and appreciated.

Another great thing about this business is that we are free to control the quality of our clients and who we want to do business with.

My intention in writing this book was to share what I have learned about the insurance business over many years. It is my hope that the ideas I have presented will help professional life insurance advisers create a legacy for their clients; a legacy of financially healthy families and financially healthy businesses.

Acknowledgments

As I said at the beginning of the book, I was lucky to make the acquaintance of the three wise men and consummate life insurance professionals: Joe Dickstein, Don Pooley, and Malcolm Scarratt.

It is a great pleasure for me to dedicate this book, with love, to Nancy, my wife of 57 years. I also would be remiss if I didn't say a special thanks to my family: my sons Marty, Mark, and Garry who are all Top of the Table Qualifiers. I also want to recognize our beloved Lee who passed away in 1993 at age 41. He is greatly missed by all our family. Then to my two daughters, Lynne, who works with us in the business and whom I look forward to seeing at the Top of the Table before too long, and Alexandra, who is an accomplished portrait artist. I would also like to say a special thank you to Alexandra for her illustrations and her contributions to this book.

It is a joy for me to recognize the other members of our large and loving family: daughters-in-law Penny, Laurie, and Lis and son-in-law Gary and my wonderful grandchildren Andrew, Chris, Joanna, Katie, Sonny, Keegan, Yolanna, Benny, Aeronn, Nikki, Jesse, Samantha, and David.

Among my greatest supporters have been my associates at Zlotnik Lamb & Company, along with the best Marketing Executive Assistant in the business, Lynn Newsome. Also, a special thank you to my Executive Assistant, Lorna Kotyk, who helps keep me on track.

I would particularly like to thank Dr. Alan Haynes, who took my rambling commentary and spent many hours organizing my thoughts into the finished product, *The Broad Concept Approach*.

Harold Zlotnik, CLU

Harold Zlotnik, CLU is a well-known lecturer and writer in the insurance industry. He has spoken five times at meetings of the Million Dollar Round Table and twice at the Top of the Table. He is a founding partner of Zlotnik, Lamb & Company, which focuses on life insurance, investment products, employee benefits, and estate and succession planning.

While serving overseas during World War II, Mr. Zlotnik flew as a navigation officer with the Royal Air Force and was awarded the Distinguished Flying Cross. In September 1945, after returning from the war, he became an insurance agent with a leading company.

Mr. Zlotnik, a life long resident of Vancouver, has been married for almost sixty years to his wife Nancy. They have three sons and two daughters. His three sons Marty, Mark, and Garry, and his daughter Lynne, are all active in the business. His younger daughter Alex is an accomplished portrait artist.

Mr. Zlotnik and his family are all active members of the Canadian Association of Family Enterprise (CAFE), which is an association of family business owners with over a thousand members across Canada. In 1995, Mr. Zlotnik produced a video on Estate and Succession Planning for CAFE. The resulting video, *Winning the Succession Game*, is now being utilized by accounting firms, law firms, and insurance agents throughout the world, to educate and motivate business owners regarding the process of estate and succession planning.

Mr. Zlotnik is very active in the Vancouver community. He is Vice-President of the Physical Medicine Research Foundation (PMRF), a worldwide medical research organization based in Vancouver, a life member of the Million Dollar Round Table, and a life member of the Top of the Table. Eight of his associates, including his three sons, qualified for the last Top of the Table and represented the largest group of qualifiers from any one marketing organization.

Zlotnik, Lamb & Co.
1200 - 666 Burrard Street
Vancouver, BC
V6C 2X8
www.zlc.net

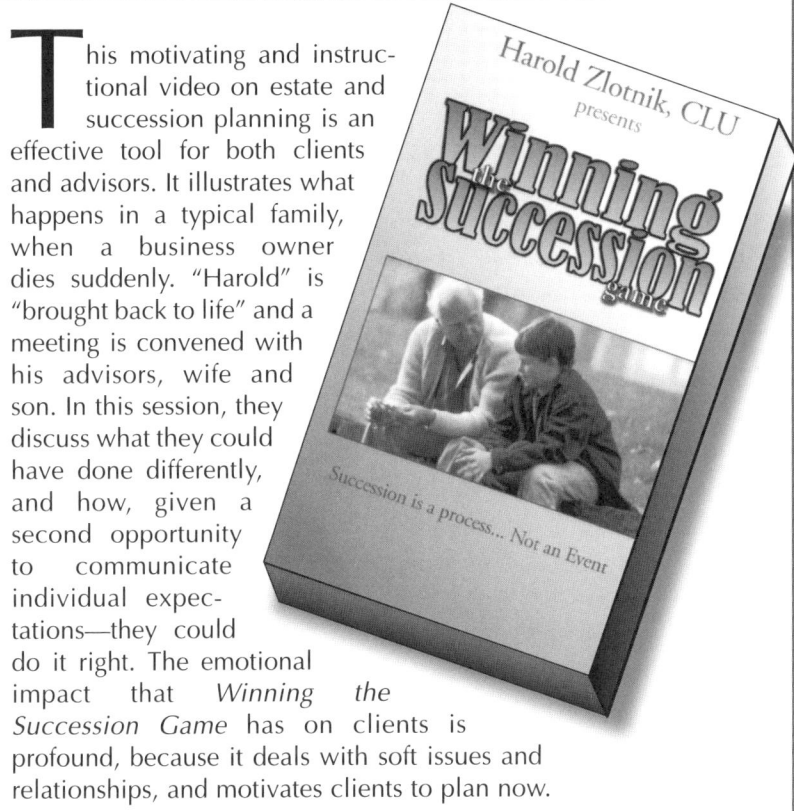

This motivating and instructional video on estate and succession planning is an effective tool for both clients and advisors. It illustrates what happens in a typical family, when a business owner dies suddenly. "Harold" is "brought back to life" and a meeting is convened with his advisors, wife and son. In this session, they discuss what they could have done differently, and how, given a second opportunity to communicate individual expectations—they could do it right. The emotional impact that *Winning the Succession Game* has on clients is profound, because it deals with soft issues and relationships, and motivates clients to plan now.

> 'It educates clients and advisors alike, and opens the door of communication. The emotional impact is profound because the client realizes their own vulnerability.'
> —DAVE McSHANE, Accountant, Managing partner KPMG, Vancouver, BC

> 'Compelling ... convincing!!!
> We recommend this high tech marketing video.'
> —RULON E. RASMUSSEN, CLU, PAST PRES., MDRT, Salt Lake City, Utah

> 'A number of my wealthy clients have received your tape with outstanding results on each occasion. The real impact is the client realizing he can no longer put off those difficult family issues. I strongly recommend your tape to all advisors in the Estate and Business Succession Planning area.'
> —GARRY AVIS, DIPAII, FLUA, TOT, Chatswood, Australia

VIDEO ORDER FORM

Winning the Succession Game Inc.,
P.O. Box 504 - 916 W. Broadway, Vancouver, B.C. Canada V5Z 1K7
Phone Toll Free: 1-877-602-4247 **Fax:** 604-224-4247 **Email:** pyoung@zlc.net
www.successionvideo.com

Print Name of person ordering _____ Print Cardholder Name _____

Print Company Name _____ Signature _____

Address _____ Province/State _____ Cardholder's Billing Address

City _____ Address _____

Zip Code _____ City _____

Phone ( ) _____ Fax ( ) _____ Province/State _____ Zip Code _____

E-Mail: _____ Regular Price: $149.00 (US Funds)
Fax or mail coupon for $20.00 off

Method of Payment: ❏ Cash ❏ Money Order   Videos requested: _____ x $129.00 = $ _____ U.S.

❏ Visa ❏ American Express   **TOTAL COST** $ _____ U.S.

Card No: _____ Exp. Date: _____